MESSAGE from the ORGANIZATION

We, the organization, wish to recognize the role of those "advertisers" in today's society who provide the ongoing boost by constantly supporting projects like this.

We sincerely appreciate and thank all the merchants, business people, and others, whose fine spirit of co-operation made it possible for us to publish and market this book.

We truly hope that you will enjoy its use. Should you require extra copies of this publication for your friends, relatives or neighbors, you may purchase them from us.

                                                    The Organization

PUBLISHED BY GATEWAY PUBLISHING CO. LTD., WINNIPEG, CANADA
    for
GATEWAY FUND RAISING SYSTEMS 811 Pandora Ave. W., Box 220 Transcona P.O., Winnipeg, Manitoba R2C 2Z9
GATEWAY FUND RAISING SYSTEMS, INC. 117 North 2nd Street, Minneapolis, Minnesota 55401

LITHO IN CANADA

Take time for 10 things

1. **Take time to Work—**
   it is the price of success.

2. **Take time to Think—**
   it is the source of power.

3. **Take time to Play—**
   it is the secret of youth.

4. **Take time to Read—**
   it is the foundation of knowledge.

5. **Take time to Worship—**
   it is the highway of reverence and washes the dust of earth from our eyes.

6. **Take time to Help and Enjoy Friends—**
   it is the source of happiness.

7. **Take time to Love—**
   it is the one sacrament of life.

8. **Take time to Dream—**
   it hitches the soul to the stars.

9. **Take time to Laugh—**
   it is the singing that helps with life's loads.

10. **Take time to Plan—**
    it is the secret of being able to have time to take time for the first nine things.

COKATO area JAYCEES
COKATO, MINNESOTA 55321
"BUILDING LEADERSHIP FOR A BETTER COMMUNITY"

What are the Jaycees?

The Jaycees is an organization for men and women between the ages of 18 and 35. It is dedicated to providing leadership training through community development. The Jaycees is designed specifically to meet the needs of the young men and women seeking to achieve personal growth and development in order to make a place for themselves in their community, in their job and in their own mind.

In working toward these goals, every young man and woman is offered the opportunities of a voice in community affairs, a practical leadership development course, the chance to try new ideas and improve old ones, and social contact with other young men and women.

Because the Jaycees take responsibility for projects, utilizing their own members, ideas, labor and follow-through, each Jaycee has the opportunity to develop their decision-making ability. Whether it is chairing a fund-raising drive, handling the publicity for a project, holding an office or chairing a standing committee, the Jaycee is being exposed to areas of knowledge and experience not gained through their occupation or profession. This exposure broadens the background of the individual Jaycee and affords valuable opportunities of the individual Jaycee for growth and leadership.

The Jaycee movement is committed to the idea that every young man or woman will be a leader of tomorrow. The Jaycees through their emphasis on personal growth and leadership training, provide an enormous pool of talent to each community for appointive or elective positions -- men and women trained by the responsibility and planning of projects and by internal development programs, men and women with public speaking ability and experience, men and women with demonstrated pride in their community and a record of community service.

WILD GAME

SUCCESS WITH SMALL GAME

The rule of punctual field care applies to small game. Immediate dressing of small game will delay spoilage caused by bacteria and animal body heat. Fortunately, too, it is easier to eviscerate and skin game animals and to pluck game birds while they are still warm.

After removing skin, cut animal open down the stomach, being sure to break the bone between the hind legs. Eviscerate it, then wipe carcass thoroughly with a clean, dry cloth or dry leaves.

Keep cool: Keep the catch cool, transport in the open air - if possible - or in a ventilated car. Once home, store meat in refrigerator, cold room or freeze after hanging. (Long delays for photography and admiration spoil many a prospective main dish before it gets to the kitchen.)

COOKING FOR FLAVOR AND TEXTURE

MEAT, GAME AND FISH

The main secrets in preparing these are to have a proper fire, good materials, and then to imprison in each dish at the outset its natural juice and characteristic flavor. Also do not over season meats, as with good materials the only seasoning needed is a little pepper and salt, which should not be added except in soups and stews, until the dish is nearly or quite done. Remember that salt draws the juices. The juices of meats and fish are their most palatable and nutritious ingredients. We extract them purposely in making soups, stews and gravies; but in so doing we spoil the meat. Fish, flesh and fowl should be cooked by first sealing the outside by searing in a very hot pan, or by plunging into boiling water. Then move further from the fire to cook gradually until done. The first process preserves the juices, and in the case of frying seals the meat or fish is a grease proof protection.

Game and all fresh meat should be hung up until it has bled thoroughly and cooled through and through. Salt meats of all kinds should be soaked overnight in cold water, or pan boiled in 2 or 3 waters before cooking. Frozen meat or fish should be soaked in ice cold water and then cooked immediately. Canned meats should at least be heated through and should never be left standing in the can. All animals from coon size down, also duck and grouse, unless young and tender, should be parboiled 10 to 30 minutes, according to size, before frying, boiling or roasting.

Meat, game and fish may be fried, boiled, roasted, baked, broiled or stewed. Frying and broiling are the quickest; roasting, baking and boiling take an hour or two; a stew of meat and vegetables, to be good, takes half a day. Tough meats (bear, procupine, etc.) should be boiled or braised in a pot.

CARE OF GAME BIRDS

Pheasant and Grouse: Draw and cool birds as soon as possible. Unhappy practice among hunters is to delay eviscerating the birds, transporting them whole in the stuffy automobile trunk. With no chance for the body heat to escape, the meat spoils.
NOTE: Showy feathers may safely be left on birds until return home.

Cleaning Tip: Pin-feathers on game birds may be removed with tweezers. Remaining feathers may be singed with a twist of lighted paper. (Avoid scorching bird's skin - and your own.)

Refrigerator Storage of Small Game:
Wrap game loosely to allow air circulation. Refrigerate in meat compartment at least 2 or 3 days before cooking. Game improves with a little aging.

Storage of Cooked Game:
Store in covered container in refrigerator. Use within 4 days.

Freezer Storage of Small Game:
Skin or pluck, draw it and cool overnight. Have the game thoroughly clean and dry. Wrap in moisture-vapor-proof material, If freezer space is limited, reserve the meatiest pieces for freezing. Store at zero degrees or lower.

IMMEDIATE, PROPER CARE OF
GAME PRECEDES GOOD DINING

Deer hunters are urged to handle their take promptly and correctly. Immediate care of the animal helps insure high quality meat.

Once the deer has been felled, the first thing to do is to bleed it. The more blood that is drained, the better the meat will keep. (Blood that remains lowers the quality of meat.) Dress the animal carefully, removing offal and wiping body cavity well. Use a dry cloth or dry leaves for this; wet meats spoils quickly.

Cool quickly. Experienced hunters recommend hanging the dressed deer in shaded spot with good air circulation. Prop flanks open with a stick 8 to 10" long, sharpened at both ends. Allow carcass to air and drain thoroughly. Disagreeable flavor usually may be traced to (1) inadequate bleeding; (2) delay or carelessness in dressing; (3) failure to cool deer at once.

COOL Transportation, too: Keep the carcass cool as possible on the trip home. Use the car top or back of a station wagon..never the hot car radiator.

To Improve Flavor: Age carcass for several days in a refrigerated or cold area. Leave skin on during aging to prevent meat from dehydrating and turning dark.

Trim the Fat: The characteristic venison flavor seems concentrated in the fat; venison fat should be completely trimmed to reduce the strong flavor. (Venison fat also turns rancid more quickly than that of domestic meat animals.)

SIGNS OF AGE

Some ways to tell the approx. age of game: Young rabbits and squirrels will be lighter in weight than older ones; their bodies will be more flexible; they will have soft, pliable ears and hard, sharp teeth.

Mature Game Birds: Their jaws are set. If you can lift the bird by its lower jaw without sign of breaking, it's an older bird.

Pheasant: Spurs on a cock pheasant are long and sharp for an old bird; the young pheasant's are blunt and pliable .. Test the breast bone of a pheasant to judge cooking time. The mature bird has stiff breast bone.

SUCCESSFUL STORAGE

Refrigeration: Like other meats, game is perishable.

Uncooked Game: - Cover or wrap loosely; use within 3 or 4 days. Organ meats and ground game should be used within 1 to 2 days.

Cooked Game: Leftover cooked game may be stored in covered container in refrigerator. Use within 3 to 4 days for best flavor.

Freezing Venison:
    Unless you have the necessary equipment and skill, it is wise to take the animal to a butcher or meat processing plant to be properly cut and wrapped. Small packages will freeze and thaw faster than large. Label all packaged game

with name of product, date frozen and weight. Freeze venison at below-zero temperatures; store at zero degrees.

Reminder: Maximum storage time for game is less than that for other meats. For best eating, use game within 4 months.

Freeze the Finest:

Deer and birds must be hung before giving them the deep freeze. No amount of hanging after they have been frozen will help. Freeze only the high quality meat.

NOTE: Cook frozen and thawed game as you would fresh game.

PREPARATION OF DUCKS

Clean well, draw, season with salt and pepper; add a tsp. of vinegar. Place in a cold water brine (about 2 tbsp. of salt to 1 qt. water) and allow to stand in a cold place overnight. Remove from the brine, dry thoroughly inside and out. Placing the bird in the salt water overnight has a tendency to remove blood clots and strong flavors.

ROASTING DUCK

Preheat oven at 550 degrees. Dry the duck and have it at room temperature. Season the inside with salt, pepper and sage. Rub salt and pepper on the outside. Put the duck on its back on a rack in the oven and leave it alone. Don't even open the door until time expires. A small duck like a teal should cook 12 to 14 mins. A mallard should cook in 20 to 22 mins. and a canvasback in a couple more mins. Use a 550 degree oven all of the time. Take it out of the oven and quarter to eat with your fingers.

ANY WILD GAME

Brains - Clean and wash in cold water. Fry or boil slowly half an hour.

Heart - Remove valves and tough, fibrous tissues; then braise or cut into small chunks and use in soups or stews.

Kidneys - Fried: Halve them, slit twice the long way on the inside but do not cut clear through; leave the fat on the kidneys. Fry until all blueness has disappeared.

Liver - Parboil the liver and skim off the scum that rises. Slice rather thin. Fry bacon and in the grease, fry the liver. Salt; add more bacon.
OR
Cut liver in slices. Soal 1 hour in cold salt water, rinse in warm water, wipe dry, dip each slice in flour seasoned with salt and pepper; fry.

Tongue - Soak for 1 hour, rinse in clean water; put in a pot of cold water, bring to a boil, simmer 2 hours or until tender. Add spices - whichever you desire.

Sausages - Utilize the tougher parts of the game by mincing raw meat with half as much salt pork, season with pepper and sage; make it into patties and fry.

Soups &

Marinades

SOUPS & MARINADES

MARINADE (MEAT)

2 tbsp. oil
2 tbsp. lemon juice
½ c. soya sauce

Combine. Pour over meat and allow to stand for 2 hours. Use sauce for basting.

MARINADE (MEAT)

4 tbsp. oil
5 tbsp. soya sauce
1 tbsp. Worcestershire sauce
tabasco sauce to taste
1 medium onion, chopped
3 tbsp. lemon juice
½ tsp. pepper

Combine ingredients and bring to a boil.

MARINADE (MEAT)

½ c. tomato catsup
3 tbsp. A-1 Sauce
2 tbsp. brown sugar
2 tbsp. vinegar
2 tbsp. oil
¼ c. water
1 tsp. salt

Combine ingredients and bring to a boil. Use sauce for basting.

MARINADE (MEAT)

½ c. red sweet wine
1 tsp. Worcestershire sauce
1 garlic clove or 2 tsp. garlic juice
1 tbsp. vinegar
¼ c. tomato catsup
1 tbsp. sugar
½ tsp. salt

Combine ingredients. Boil. Cool. Marinate meat in sauce.

* EXTRA RECIPES *

HERB STEAK MARINADE

3 lb. chuck or round steak 1½" thick
2 tbsp. Worcestershire sauce
1½ tsp. meat tenderizer
¼ tsp. rosemary
Marinate ½ hour

¼ c. vinegar (or wine vinegar)
2 tbsp. salad oil
¼ tsp. marjoram
¼ tsp. tyme (crushed)

GAME SOUP

Soup bone - a leg joint with some meat on it is best. Boil in large pot for about 5 or 6 hrs. or until meat is leaving bone. Then add grated or diced carrots, onions, celery if you have it, a hand full or two of rice, salt and pepper to taste. Cook till rice is done. Other vegetables and macaroni may also be used and you may like to add tabasco or HP sauce.

DUCK SOUP

1 large or small 2 ducks (cut into small pieces)
8 c. water
2 stalks celery with leaves, chopped
1 large onion, diced
1 tsp. salt
6 chicken bouillon cubes

Place all in a large pot. Simmer gently for 2 or 3 hrs. If too thick, add 1 c. water. Add 2 to 3 oz. of thin noodles. Cook very slowly half an hr. longer and serve.

ELK SOUP

2½ to 3 lb. knuckle bone and meat
1 large onion - quartered
1 c. diced carrots
¼ tsp. pepper

2 tsp. parsley
2 quarts water
¾ c. diced celery
4 tsp. salt
⅓ c. rice

Saw or crack bone in several pieces. Wipe pieces clean with damp cloth. Put into soup kettle and add water. Heat to boiling. Reduce heat, cover and simmer gently for 2 to 2½ hours. Remove bone, cut off meat and dice. Return meat and marrow to soup, add remaining ingredients and simmer 20 to 30 minutes, until rice and vegetables are done. Serve 4 - 6.

CLAM CHOWDER

Peel and grate 4 large potatoes into a heavy deep kettle. Add enough water so that potatoes can simmer slowly without sticking. Add 3 cans baby clams. Meanwhile cut up fine 1 c. bacon ends or ham ends, 1 c. onions. Put bacon and onions together in a skillet and cook slowly till cooked lightly. Drain off fat. Add onions and bacon to potatoes. Add 1 c. cream or 2 c. milk. Salt and pepper to taste and add ½ c. margarine. Simmer slowly for ½ hr., stirring often. I make potato soup by using the same method, omitting the clams.

CLAM CHOWDER SOUP

Dice - 6 or 8 slices bacon   2 c. potatoes
1 med. onion

Fry bacon until crisp, take out and dry on paper towel. Cook onions lightly in bacon fat. Meanwhile cook diced potatoes in small amount of water for 20 min. or until tender. Add bacon, onion, 1 or 2 cans small clams, 6 or 8 c. powdered milk, pinch of celery salt, salt and pepper to taste. Paprika (optional). Heat and serve.

FISH CHOWDER FOR 5

6 perch gutted and beheaded
Scald fish and skin
Boil about 7 min. and debone
2 large potatoes, cooked — mash one - cube one
3 stalks celery — 1 med. onion
diced and cooked separately with salt

Combine in one pot, add marjoram, salt, pepper, milk to cover. Simmer 15 -20 minutes.

CATFISH SOUP

2 to 3 lbs. of catfish, cut up
1 chopped celery stalk
Herbs (bay leaf, parsley thyme)
2 qts. cold water
1 sliced onion
salt and pepper
1 c. milk
2 tbsp. butter

Place all ingredients into a stew pan and put on a slow fire. Stir occasionally and cook until the fish readily falls to pieces. Serve hot.

FISH CHOWDER

1 c. salt pork or bacon, diced
2 c. hot water
Salt and Pepper
2 c. half & half cream
¾ c. sliced onions
2 c. diced potatoes
1½ lbs. fish fillets, such as walleye, perch or pickerel
Butter

Fry the salt pork in a skillet until it is nicely browned. Add the onions and saute them gently. Add the potatoes and hot water and cook them for a few mins. or until the potatoes are partly done. Then add the fish fillets and cook until they are easily flaked with a fork. Season to taste with salt and pepper; add cream. Let is all heat thoroughly and serve in bowls, topping with a pat of butter.

TURTLE SOUP

3 lbs. turtle meat, cut small
4 tbsp. flour
1 tbsp. salt
4 qts. stock & water
2 bay leaves
6 cloves
2 tbsp. lemon juice
4 tbsp. fat
1 c. tomatoes
½ clove garlic, minced fine
1 lump sugar
2 sprigs parsley
½ tsp. mace

Parboil meat for 10 mins.; save water for stock. Fry meat in fat. Remove meat from pan and brown the flour. Add tomatoes, salt and garlic. Add remaining ingredients and bring to a boil. Add turtle meat. Cook 3 hrs. Strain if desired.

SNAPPING TURTLE SOUP

1 large snapping turtle

Use an ax to chop off head and with shell upside down use ax to remove top from bottom. Using a very sharp knife, skin out legs, neck and tail. Cook in water slowly as rapid cooking toughens the meat. Simmer about 3 hrs. Remove meat from bones and now make your favorite homemade vegetable soup. Use the heart and liver in the soup.

PHEASANT SOUP

Pheasant bones, skin and left over meat
>Parsley
>1 bay leaf
>2 carrots, chopped
>Celery leaves, chopped
>Chicken stock (opt.)
>¼ c. sherry wine
>Thyme
>1 small onion, chopped
>1 to 2 whole cloves
>Salt to taste
>2 to 3 peppercorns, crushed

Combine left over pheasant with a few sprigs of parsley and thyme; add bay leaf, onion, carrots, cloves, celery leaves, salt and peppercorns. Barely cover with water or ½ water and ½ chicken broth; simmer for 2 hrs. Strain broth; add sherry. Serve with melba toast, if desired. Yield: 4 servings.

Wild Meats

WILD MEATS

SWISS STEAK — TRAIL STYLE

This can be made with any game meat and if the animal should be a little tough, just cook it in the oven longer.

Cut steak not too thick, about ½". Roll in well seasoned flour and brown on both sides but not necessary to cook very much. Place in roasting pan (or large pot if on the trail). (We cook a large quantity as it is good warmed over), slice a large onion or two and some celery if you have it, mix with meat. Pour over this a can of tomato juice and 1 or 2 cans of tomatoes depending on the amount of meat you have. Add enough water to bring liquid to top of meat. Then bake until meat is cooked. This usually takes about an hour but longer if meat is a bit tough. Salt and pepper to taste. This can also be made with mushroom or celery soup. Just add 2 or 3 cans of mushroom or celery soup and water in place of tomato.

SWISS STEAK

2 lbs. swiss or round steak
¾ c. flour
2 c. sliced onions
2 tbsp. fat (Note- this applies to beef only moose use ½ c.)
2 tsp. salt
¼ tsp. pepper
1 clove garlic chopped fine (or 1 tsp. garlic salt or powder)
½ c. water
1 tbsp. dry mustard
1 c. chili sauce or cooked tomatoes

Pound flour into steak - fry onions in fat. Remove onions. Brown steak on both sides. Cover with onions - add mustard, salt, pepper, garlic, water and chili sauce or tomatoes. Cover and cook over low heat or bake in oven at 350 for

Beef - 1½ to 2 hours
Moose - 2-2½ hours.

SWISS STEAK IN SOUR CREAM

(with or without vegetables) serves 6.
Three lbs. round steak cut into serving pieces. Dredge meat in flour seasoned

with salt and pepper. Melt ⅓ c. shortening in large skillet or roasting pan. Brown meat on both sides. Lower heat, cover and simmer. Lay 1 slice onion on each piece of meat. Pour over all 1½ to 2 c. sour cream. Cover tightly and bake at 300 about 2 hrs. (more depending on thickness of steaks). Carrots, potatoes, parsnips cut in halves and mushrooms whole or pieces may be added before baking for a complete meal in one pot. Serve with rice or noodles if no vegetables have been added.

PEPPER STEAK

Cut 1½ lbs. of beef, moose, sheep, etc., round steak cut ½" thick in strips. Coat with mixture of ¼ c. flour, ½ tsp. salt, 1/8 tsp. pepper. In large skillet, brown strips in hot shortening. Drain one 8 oz. can tomatoes, reserving liquid. Add reserved liquid, 1-¾ c. water, ½ c. chopped onion, 1 small clove garlic, minced and 1 tbsp. beef flavored gravy base to meat. Cover, simmer 1¼ hrs. or until meat is tender, uncover and stir in 1½ tsp. Worcestershire sauce. Cut 2 large green peppers in strips and add to meat. Cover and simmer meat and green peppers for 5 min. If gravy is too thin, combine 1 or 2 tbsp. flour with water and stir into sauce. Cook and stir till thick and bubbly. Add drained tomatoes cut up and cook for 5 min. more. Serve over hot cooked rice. Serves 6.

STEAK AND MILK GRAVY

Cut steaks ½" thick (wild meat is best). Roll each steak in flour. Cook in heavy pan in bacon drippings or margarine until steaks are well seared on both sides. I have my pan quite hot with quite a bit of fat in it. As the steaks cook, put them in a foil covered pan to keep hot. In the pan that the steaks were cooked in, add more fat, ½ c. of flour, and stir till all the steak drippings are well loosened in the pan. Do not let your flour get brown. Have a quart of powdered milk ready beforehand. As soon as the flour and fat are well mixed in the steak pan, slowly pour the milk in, mixing all the time. As soon as gravy starts to thicken turn heat down and let it slowly simmer. Add salt and pepper to taste. Do not over boil or the gravy will curdle. This is a good trail meal as it can be done over a camp fire or trail stove in a hurry and served with hot biscuits, bannock or bread. Is a good hot meal.

STEAK AND GRAVY

Use all the tougher steaks of moose and deer, also caribou, by browning. Add a tin of cream of mushroom soup. Simmer about 1 hr. after browning. Use with mashed potatoes, rice or macaroni. Raw onion may be added if you like some before simmering.

TRIUMPHANT MOOSE (ELK, VENISON) STEAKS

1½ lb. steak	1 c. sliced onion
1 tbsp. mustard	1 diced carrot
4 tbsp. cornstarch	1½ c. tomatoes
½ tsp. salt	¼ tsp. pepper

Nick edges of steak. Mix dry ingredients. Pound into both sides of steak. Sear steak, cover with onions, carrots, tomatoes and bake covered 1½ hrs. Serve with oven browned potatoes and baked apples.

OVEN BARBECUED STEAKS

3 lbs. round steak (good on tough steak)	½ c. chopped onion
2 tbsp. oil	½ c. vinegar
¾ c. ketchup	1 tbsp. brown sugar
¾ c. water	½ tsp. salt
1 tbsp. prepared mustard	1 tbsp. Worcestershire sauce
	1/8 tsp. pepper

Brown steaks in hot oil. Remove steaks to bake pan. Brown onions slightly, add remaining ingredients and simmer 5 min. Pour over steaks. Cook in oven for 2 hrs.

DEER, MOOSE OR CARIBOU CUTLETS OR STEAK

Use round steak cut thin, also front leg lower below shoulder for cutlets. Dip in 2 beaten eggs and roll in 1 or 2 packets of salted cracker crumbs. Fry in cooking oil or Crisco until brown on both sides.

BREADED CUTLETS

As many steaks as needed
1 c. milk and 1 egg beaten together
Fine cracker crumbs
Flour
Salt and pepper

Pound steaks and sprinkle lightly on both sides with salt and pepper. Roll in flour, dip in egg mixture and roll in cracker crumbs. Fry until desired doneness. This will keep the bread on the cutlets and works well on any game meat.

BRAISED VENISON

2 c. flour	2 tbsp. fat
1 tsp. salt	¾ c. onion rings
½ tsp. pepper	Garlic salt
8 venison steaks	2 c. water

Sift dry ingredients except garlic salt. Coat venison with dry ingredients. Brown in fat. Top with onion rings; sprinkle with garlic salt. Add water; simmer for 1 hr. over med. heat. Yield: 8 servings.

BARBECUED OVEN STEAK

Trim from wild game steaks, any fat. Lay steaks on board, sprinkle surface with salt, pepper and garlic salt. Pound meat with edge of saucer, turn meat over and repeat. Let stand ½ hour. Brown steaks in greased fry pan.

Barbecue Sauce:

1 can tomato soup	1 large chopped onion
3 to 4 c. water	1 c. chopped celery
2 tbsp. brown sugar	½ tsp. dried mustard
2 tbsp. vinegar	2 tsp. cornstarch
1 clove crushed garlic	½ tsp. salt

Combine ingredients. Place browned steaks in roaster and pour sauce over them. Bake in 350 degree oven until done.

BREADED VENISON STEAKS IN WINE

4-8 venison round steaks
1 egg, beaten
1 c. cracker crumbs
½ c. flour
Salt and pepper
4 tbsp. cooking oil
1 onion, chopped
1 can mushrooms, drained
1 c. red wine

Dip steaks in egg, roll in mixture of cracker crumbs, flour, salt and pepper. Brown steaks in oil, place in baking dish. Cover with onion, mushrooms, and wine. Bake, covered at 350 degrees for 1 hour and 30 minutes.

DEER CHILI

4 lbs. meat, ground
5 cloves minced garlic
5 tbsp. chili powder
2½ tbsp. paprika
1½ tbsp. comino seeds
1 tbsp. salt
1 tbsp. white pepper
2 quarts water

First get your deer. Brown meat in a small amount of grease in a kettle, add garlic, chili powder, paprika, comino seeds, salt and pepper. (This is a man's dish - for Ladies with milder tastes, use less pepper). Stir in 2 quarts of water. Cover and cook slowly, stirring occasionally, about 3 hours. If more water is needed during cooking, add 1 c. at a time, it may be served as is or with equal parts cooked pink beans or red kidney beans. Makes 3½ quarts.

WEIGHT WATCHERS CHILI & CHOP SUEY

1 lb. ground beef or venison
1 can bean sprouts
1 can french cut beans
1 large can tomato juice
1 can mushrooms
1 small onion
Salt
Pepper
Chili Powder

For Chop Suey:
    Eliminate part of tomato juice and chili powder
    Add soya sauce.

Brown meat and drain. Combine ingredients and simmer until thickened. Serve over rice.

SUKIYAKI

1 lb. wild meat or beef
½ head cabbage, sliced thin
1 large onion sliced & broken apart
5 stalks celery, sliced in strips

1 can cream of mushroom soup
4 tbsp. soy sauce
1 can bean sprouts
1 can mushroom pieces

Cut meat in thin strips. Fry till brown in a little fat. Remove. Add onions, celery, and cabbage and cook till near done. Add to meat. Add soup and juice from bean sprouts. Cook for 15 min. Add soy sauce and bean sprouts. Serve with rice.

MINESTRONE DINNER

2-3 lbs. boiling meat with some good beef fat helps the flavour
2 tbsp. salt
½ c. onions (diced)
1-2 c. dry red kidney beans, water to cover

Salt and pepper to taste
1½ c. broken spaghetti
1 minced onion
1 lb. ground meat

Vegetables - celery, cabbage, carrots, squash, peas, string beans, canned tomatoes or what have you.

Cook first 6 ingredients about 3 hrs., adding more water when needed. Cool and remove any bones and most of the fat. Cut up any large pieces of meat. Saute next 3 ingredients and add to first part, along with longer cooking vegetables, simmer. Add spaghetti and quicker cooking vegetables about 20 min. before serving time. Use your own variations and quantities of vegetables and spices. I don't think I ever made this the same twice.

HOBO DINNER

Season hamburger and brown in a frying pan. Put in the bottom of a casserole dish. Cover with layers of sliced onions, carrots, potatoes and cheese slices, adding salt and pepper to vegetables. Cover and bake in 300 degree oven until vegetables are done.

GAMEBURGER CASSEROLE

Take 2 or 3 lbs. of ground meat from any game animal and brown a little in pan. Then put in casserole. Slice 1 onion on this and fill casserole with thinly sliced raw potatoes. Salt and pepper. Over this pour 1 or 2 cans of cream of mushroom or cream of celery soup. Bake till potatoes are tender.

PIQUANT MEAT LOAF

¾ c. dry bread crumbs
1 c. milk
1½ lb. ground meat
1 onion, chopped and parboiled
2 eggs, slightly beaten
1 tsp. salt
¼ tsp. pepper
½ tsp. sage or poultry seasoning

Soak crumbs in milk add meat, eggs, onions and seasonings. Pack lightly in greased loaf pan. Spread with sauce and bake from 1 hr. to 1¼ hrs. at 350 degrees.

SAUCE combine 4 tbsp. brown sugar, 5 tbsp. ketchup, ½ tsp. nutmeg, 1½ tsp. dry mustard. Pour over meat loaf.

DINNER IN A ROLL

2 c. ground meat
2 tbsp. chopped parsley
¾ tsp. salt
2 tbsp. water or tomato juice
½ onion, minced
1 tbsp. melted butter
¼ tsp. pepper
Biscuit dough

Make a dough as for biscuits adding ½ c. mashed potatoes to flour when mixing. Roll out. Spread with the meat filling. Roll up as for jelly roll. Bake in a very hot oven, 450 degrees for 30 min. Either cooked or uncooked meat can be used.

POT LUCK CASSEROLE

2 med. onions, chopped
13 oz. extra sharp cheese, grated
2 cans cream of chicken soup
1 can mushroom soup
4 c. cooked rice
½ c. slivered and buttered browned almonds
3 lbs. ground meat
1 can mushroom buttons and juice
Shredded cabbage and green pepper

Brown onion, add meat and brown, salt lightly, add rest of ingredients. Cover with chinese noodles and bake in large Dutch oven or in two casseroles at 350 degrees for 30 min. This recipe can be halved. It can also be frozen and reheated.

VENISON OR MOOSE CABBAGE ROLLS

12 large cabbage leaves
1½ lb. ground moose or deer meat
4 tbsp. grated onion
½ c. butter
1½ c. cooked rice
2 tbsp. chopped dill
3 c. canned tomato sauce
1 tbsp. salt
Pepper to taste

Brown meat and onion in butter. Mix in the rice, dill, salt and pepper. Place cabbage leaves in boiling water for 1 min., drain and dry. Place meat mixture in center of leaves and fold over, securing with a toothpick. Place the works in shallow baking dish - pour tomato sauce over. Cover and bake at 325 degrees for 45 min.

SURPRISE MEATBALLS

1 lb. ground venison
½ lb. ground pork
½ tsp. salt
Dash of pepper
¼ c. cream
2 c. toasted bread cubes
4 tbsp. onion, chopped
1 tbsp. parsley, chopped
3 tbsp. butter
1 tsp. poultry seasoning
3 tbsp. fat
1 10½ oz. can cream of mushroom soup
¾ c. milk

Combine meat, salt, pepper and cream. Form meat into 20 patties. Mix bread cubes, onion, parsley, 3 tbsp. melted butter and seasonings together. Place stuffing on 10 patties. Cover with remaining patties and form into ball - being careful to seal in stuffing. Brown meatballs in hot fat. Add mushroom soup mixed in milk. Cook 30 to 45 mins., covered. Serves 4-6.

VENISON MEAT BALLS

2 c. grated raw potatoes	¼ c. milk
1½ lb. ground venison	¼ c. butter
1 tbsp. chopped onion	3 c. water
1½ tsp. salt	2 to 3 tbsp. flour
1/8 tsp. pepper	2 c. sour cream
1 egg	1 tsp. dill seed

Combine potatoes, venison, onion, salt, pepper, egg and milk; shape into 1½" balls. Brown balls slowly in butter in large skillet. Add ½ c. water; cover. Simmer for 20 mins. or until done. Remove meatballs. Stir in flour and remaining water; simmer until thick. Reduce heat; stir in cream and dill. Add meatballs; heat, but do not boil. NOTE: May be cooked by alternate method. Brown meatballs; remove to casserole. Make gravy; add sour cream and dill. Pour gravy over meatballs and finish in oven. Yield: 8 servings.

VENISON BURGER

(Over an open fire)

Aluminum foil	Butter
Salt and pepper to taste	Onion

Wrap each venison burger patty in heavy duty aluminum foil together with a slice of onion, 1 tbsp. of butter and salt and pepper. Place the wrapped patties right in the red coals of an outdoor hardwood fire. Let 'em sizzle for 10 mins. without turning. Keep the juice in by keeping the folded edge on top. Toast a hamburger roll while you wait and add some ketchup to the results if you like.

LEG OF VENISON

5 to 6 lbs. venison	3 tbsp. tarragon vinegar
½ c. brown sugar	1 tsp. allspice
2½ c. salad oil	1 tsp. salt
¼ c. lemon juice	1 tsp. lemon rind, grated

Bring to boiling point and simmer 15 mins. Let cool before inserting meat. Marinate in refrigerator 24 to 26 hrs. Bake at 325 degrees until done. During baking, baste every 30 mins. When done, can be placed in outer smoker and smoked for 2 to 3 hrs. to give it extra flavor.

VENISON ROAST

1-5 lb. boneless rump venison roast
½ lb. salt pork
cornstarch
1 quart buttermilk
½ c. orange juice

Soak meat in buttermilk in plastic bag in a bowl for 3 days at room temperature. Turn bag 2 times a day. Remove meat. Cut salt pork into ½ x 1 inch pieces. Pierce meat with sharp knife every inch, force salt pork into slits. Roast 3 hours at 350 degrees. (Venison cannot be served rare or medium). Add water to drippings to make 3 cups. Add orange juice, thicken gravy with cornstarch for a smooth mixture. Yield: 10 to 12 servings.
*Buttermilk tenderizes the meat.

VENISON ROAST

Leg or saddle of venison
Bacon
Equal parts dry white wine, vinegar and water.
3 pieces lemon
6 cloves
1 small cinnamon stick
2 bay leaves
3 carrots
¼ bunch parsley
½ tsp. pepper
pinch of rosemary
1 cut up onion

Remove surplus skin and fibers from venison. Using a larding needle lard heavily with bacon. Bring rest of ingredients to a boil, pour over meat and let stand 1 day in roasting pan. If meat is not covered by marinade, turn occasionally. Remove meat and brown on all sides. Heat marinade in pan, add meat, cover and bake at 400 degrees about 3 hours, basting often. If marinade is plentiful, use only part for roasting, adding marinade during cooking and to gravy. Remove meat and keep warm. Mix ½ c. sweet or sour cream with flour. Stir into pan juices until thick. Add a bit of lemon or orange juice, sugar, and salt. Strain gravy, slice meat and serve with potato balls, red cabbage, and cranberry sauce. Makes 6 servings.

KEAVENY PHARMACY

THOMAS KEAVENY, R. Ph.

COKATO, MN.   **PHONE 286-5618**

Hallmark ♔ *Cards*   *Fanny Farmer* FAMOUS CANDIES

COMPLETE LINE OF GIFTS & COSMETICS

Win Brand Jewelry

GIFTS — CHINA — JEWELRY — WATCHES
BRIDAL REGISTRY
SPECIAL ORDER JEWELRY & DIAMOND SETTING
— Win Brand, Jeweler —

210 BROADWAY   **TELEPHONE: (612) 286-2451**   **COKATO, MN.**

COKATO
Bakery & Coffee Shop

BREADS - ROLLS - PASTRIES
Fresh Daily
WEDDING SPECIALTIES - BIRTHDAY CAKES

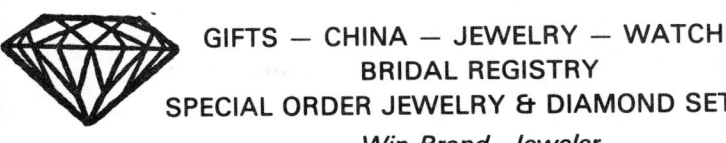

200 Broadway Ave.   **COKATO, MN.**   **286-5614**

Please Patronize Our Advertisers

SWANSON & PETERSON

Furniture Store
Funeral Home

Cokato, Mn.   286-2534

"Serving this community since 1902"

— TOTAL HARDWARE — **Coast to Coast**

DEL & NORMA RAASCH

Phone 286-2812
COKATO, MINNESOTA 55321

COKATO CHIROPRACTIC OFFICE

HEALTH thru CHIROPRACTIC

DR. Steven Rosenbluth, Chiropractor

310 MILLARD AVENUE, COKATO, MN 55321
Phone: 286-5734

THE SOCIETY OF PROFESSIONAL SALES COUNSELORS

HOLT MOTOR, INC.

COKATO, MN.
PHONE: 286-2176

LITCHFIELD, MN.
PHONE: 693-7937

ROAST VENISON

Preferably a neck roast or rump roast
1 pkg. Lipton's onion soup
Salt and pepper   Parsley flakes
Garlic powder   Sweet basil

Wash and clean the meat. Wrap up tightly in heavy foil after you have seasoned same with all ingredients. Roast in a heavy roasting pan for 2-3 hours in 325 degree oven.

ROAST SADDLE OF VENISON

The saddle is the double loin, which includes the two loins joined at the backbone. It is a choice cut. Cover the meat with thinly sliced bacon and tie on with a string. Put in a roasting pan with two sliced onions, 2 sliced carrots, 4 diced slices of bacon and 2 tbsp. butter. Roast in a very hot oven (450 degrees) for 15 min. reduce heat to 325 and roast until meat thermometer reads 140. Serve with sauce below.

SAUCE - cook 2 c. venison stock until it has been reduced to 1 c. Add ½ c. chopped sauted mushrooms, ½ c. sauted venison liver, ¼ c. port wine and 2 tbsp. each of butter and flour (blended until smooth). Simmer 15 min., add 1 tsp. lemon juice to the sauce just before serving.

PICKLED VENISON WITH CREAM GRAVY

Venison roast   10 whole allspice
Salt   1 bay leaf
1½ c. vinegar   Lemon rind
3 c. water   1-⅓ c. sour cream
1 large onion, sliced   1 tsp. flour
6 whole cloves   1 egg yolk, beaten

Trim venison roast and dust with salt. Combine vinegar, 2 c. water, onion, spices. Cover and boil 15 min. Then let cool and pour over venison roast. Let marinate for 2 or 3 days, turning once or twice each day. When ready to bake, place in a baking pan and add about ½ of the marinade, remaining cup of water and piece of lemon rind. Bake in 325 degree oven for 25 to 30 min. per lb. When half done baste with ½ c. sour cream. Turn over once while baking and baste frequently. When done, remove roast. Add remaining sour cream to liquid. Thicken with flour and beaten egg yolk. Strain sauce and serve with potatoes or dumplings.

SMOKED VENISON

Electric smoker
Salt and pepper
Molasses
Cheesecloth

5-10 lbs. lean venison meat
Brown sugar
Vinegar
Woodchips (hickory, hard maple, apple, cherry)

Cut meat into strips 6 to 8" long and no more than ½" thick, and 1 to 2" wide. Soak meat in a salt water and vinegar brine solution overnight in a deep bowl or crock. Mix 1 c. salt and ½ c. brown sugar in flat pan. (Cake pan or cookie sheet). Dredge meat in salt and sugar and rub well into meat. Next, rub ½ tsp. of molasses on each meat strip and then roll entire quantity of prepared meat in cheesecloth or similiar type cloth. Place in a cool place for 4 to 5 hrs. Rinse excess salt off from meat with cold water after previous time allowance. If the salt is not rinsed off, the meat will be too salty to eat. After the salt is rinsed off, dry each piece of meat on paper towels. Next, sprinkle black pepper sparingly on the strips. Your meat is now ready to smoke.
(Rubbing a small amount of molasses and brown sugar into meat again will give it a sweeter taste after smoking). Place meat on racks in smoker and smoke meat from 5 to 8 hrs., depending on taste. Check woodchips every hr. to keep meat under a constant smoke.
(NOTE: If it is found that meat is still too salty after smoking, then the meat wasn't rinsed well enough in cold water. Simply take remaining unsmoked meat and soak in cold water for about an hr. This should do the trick.)

VENISON STEW

Time - 3 to 4 hrs.

5 qt. kettle (Dutch Oven)
2½ qt. water
3 med. carrots, diced
1 stalk celery, diced
3 small onions, diced

5 med. potatoes, diced
3 to 4 lbs. venison
1½ tsp. salt
1/8 tsp. pepper

Remove meat from bone; cut in 1½" cubes. Put meat in kettle; boil until tender. Then remove meat from kettle and put on plate. (This prevents meat from being over cooked). Add vegetables to hot liquid and cook until tender. Then put meat back in kettle and make gravy, by thickening liquid with flour.

Then turn stew down to simmer and serve in bowls or over Baking Powder Biscuits.

BAKING POWDER BISCUTS

Large Recipe - 24 biscuits	Half recipe - 12 biscuits
4 c. (1 qt.) sifted flour	2 c. sifted flour
5 tsp. baking powder	2½ tsp. baking powder
½ tsp. salt	1/8 tsp. salt
½ c. shortening	4 tbsp. shortening
1⅓ c. milk (about)	⅔ c. milk (about)

Sift flour once; measure; add baking powder and salt and sift together into bowl. Cut in shortening until mixture looks like coarse meal, using 2 knives or a wire pastry blender. Add milk, mixing until a soft dough is formed. Turn dough onto a lightly floured board and knead half a min. to shape. (Takes about 15 turns). Roll or pat ½" thick. Cut with floured 2" cutter. Let stand undisturbed for another ½ min., if you want especially even, well shaped biscuits! Place on ungreased baking sheet. Bake in hot oven, 450 degrees F. for 12 to 15 mins.

FOR-QUICK-BISCUITS, increase milk to 2 c. for large recipe, 1 c. for the half recipe. Mix dough and drop from tsp. onto sheet or greased muffin pans. Bake.

DIFFERENT VENISON STEW

The first step is to make a marinade that has been simmered. In a large saucepan, mix:

1½ c. vinegar	¾ c. vegetable oil
2 or 3 slices of onion	A pared and diced carrot
1 large or 2 small cloves of garlic, peeled and crushed	1 tsp. thyme
	12 black peppercorns
	2 cloves
A large bay leaf	1 tbsp. salt

Enough water to cover the meat along with the other ingredients.
Bring the mixture to a boil and simmer for 15 mins. for a tenderizing marinade. If the meat used (3 lbs. is a good amount) is cold, cover it immediately with the marinade. If the meat is at room temp., chill the marinade first. If no cool place is available, refrigerate the meat in the marinade overnight to prevent spoilage. Next day, drain the marinade into a bowl and disard any bits of meat that are gristly. Dry the meat on paper towels and sear it in a Dutch oven with corn or peanut oil.

Cast-iron utensils work well. Do not crowd the pieces.
Set the meat aside in a bowl when searing is completed. Lower the heat; add oil, a bit of butter and sliced carrots and small onions as desired. Gently brown the mixture over low heat. Add a bit of brown sugar, if desired. Return the meat to the Dutch oven with the vegetables; sprinkle with enough flour to coat each piece and heat, stirring until the flour is set. Add the marinade, some fresh parsley and enough water and dry red wine to just cover. Simmer over low heat until very tender, stirring now and then. When reheated the next day, super leftovers result.

VENISON SUMMER SAUSAGE

Grind together:
    4 lbs. pork
    12 lb. venison - choice meat without cords

Add:
    3 heaping tbsp. Tenderquick ½ c. smoke salt
    3 tsp. pepper 1 tsp. liquid smoke
    3 tbsp. whole mustard seed

Mix thoroughly. Let stand in cool place overnight. Cover to avoid drying on top. Use sausage stuffer to stuff in casings. Tie shut and let stand in cool place overnight. (Don't freeze). Smoke for about 4 hrs. Let smoke draw in overnight. Smoke again for about 4 hrs. or to taste. Smoke will draw in. Stand again for a day. Store in freezer.

VENISON SAUSAGE

10 lbs. meat (5 lbs. venison and 5 lbs. pork)
    7 tsp. salt (or ½ c) 2-3 cloves of garlic,
    ¼ c. pepper minced fine

Grind all together. Pack in sausage casing or use as bulk.

HEART OF VENISON

    1 deer heart 1 bay leaf
    5 strips of bacon ½ tsp. sweet basil
    1 pt. tomato juice 5 whole cloves
    1 pt. water Pinch cinnamon

Place tomato juice, water and spices in the bottom of a steamer kettle. In top of steamer, place the heart with the bacon strips on top. Cover tightly and steam slowly for 3 hrs. or until fork inserted in the meat comes out easily. Chill the heart thoroughly, then slice thin and serve cold. Strain the cooking liquid from this and use as a base for venison stew.

VENISON TIDBITS

Bacon
Venison
2 c. water

Salt
Black pepper
½ c. Worcestershire sauce

Cut pieces of venison into 1" squares. Take a thin slice of bacon and cut it just long enough to wrap around the meat. Secure with a toothpick. Make about 2 dozen. Put in a cast-iron skillet. Add 2 c. water, salt, lots of black pepper, and ½ c. Worcestershire sauce. Boil rapidly until water is nearly gone. Reduce heat and cover skillet. Continue cooking at lower temp. until meat is brown. The meat will be very rich.

RINGALLS (MEAT CAKES)

2-3 lb. venison
¼ lb. salt pork

Salt & pepper to taste
¼ c. chopped onion

Chop meat, pork and onion into small pieces. Add salt and pepper. To above mixture add enough flour to make a batter to the consistency of thick pan cakes, and drop by tablespoon in deep fat. Brown well on both sides. This mixture can be made thick enough to form into patties, or it can be put in a loaf pan and baked as a meat loaf. This can be served with any vegetable you desire.

ROLLED MOOSE STEAKS

2 lbs. moose steak cut ¼" thick
   ¾ c. flour
   ½ tsp. salt
   1½ c. sage dressing

¼ tsp. pepper
1 c. water
Dash of sweet marjoram, rosemary, thyme

Cut the moose into 2"x4" slices and pound flour salt and pepper well into each piece. Next place a mound of sage dressing in the centre of each slice and fold the moose meat over the stuffing and fasten with a toothpick. Place in the roaster and add water and herbs and bake for 1 hr. Letting it brown well before serving.

MOOSE STEAK SUPREME

Moose steak
Cracker crumbs
1 egg
¼ c. milk
Salt and pepper

Cut moose steak very thin. Pound on both sides to tenderize. Beat egg, milk and seasoning in a small bowl. Dip meat in egg mixture, then dip in cracker crumbs. Fry meat in medium hot pan.

MOOSE TENDERLOIN CASSEROLE

8-12 pieces flattened tenderloin
4 med. sized onions, chopped
chopped green pepper
1 tin cream of mushroom soup
Seasoning

Fry onions and green pepper lightly. Flour and season the tenderloin and brown lightly. Drain off any excess frying fat. Place meat and vegetables in casserole and cover with mushroom soup and 1 c. of water. Cook in moderate oven for about 1 hr. or until tender.

MOOSE STEW

Melt several tbsp. bacon grease in heavy pan. Dip chunks of moose meat in seasoned flour and brown in bacon grease. Add boiling water to almost cover meat, and simmer 2½ to 3 hrs. Add in the following order - 1 med. turnip cut in small cubes, 10-12 potatoes, 6 carrots, 1 sliced onion. Cook until barely tender, seasoning to taste. Thicken gravy with a little flour mixed with cold water. If desired, add dumplings during last 15 min. of cooking (before thickening gravy).

Dumplings:

1½ c. flour	1 tsp. sugar
2¼ tsp. baking powder	3 tbsp. margarine
¾ tsp. salt	about ¾ c. milk

Sift dry ingredients. Cut in shortening. Add milk to make a thick drop batter. Make sure there is still plenty of liquid in stew. Drop dumpling mixture on top of meat and vegetables with a tbsp. Cover the pot tightly and steam for 15 min. without lifting the cover.

MAYBELLES MOOSE

1 lb. ground moose	¼ lb. ground salt pork
3 tbsp. butter	1 small minced onion
1½ c. spaghetti	1 large can tomatoes
1 small can peas	1 small can pimentoes
1 small can olives	½ lb. grated cheese

Melt butter in a large frying pan and lightly saute minced onions, add ground meat and cook until done. Meanwhile cook the spaghetti in boiling water adding salt and drain. Also drain tomatoes and peas add to meat. Place ½ in a casserole and sprinkle with cheese, add the other half and top with cracker crumbs. Bake for 45 mins.

DUTCH OVEN RIBS

Cook well, slowly 5 or 6 hrs. if moose is tough. Salt and pepper, onion, barbecue sauce and a little water in Dutch oven.

MOOSEBURGER STEAK

Grind 5 lbs. lean meat and 1 lb. suet. (kidney fat). Soak 3 slices of bread. Do not squeeze water out of the bread. Add wet bread to the meat. Chop large onion fine. Add to meat. Salt and pepper and either one finely chopped clove of garlic or garic salt. Mix well in large pan. Make into either large steaks or small patties. Cook over medium hot heat. These could be served with mushrooms or fried onions or just plain.

BACK STRAP ROAST

Soak a back strap in half and half of water and vinegar for 10 min. Then drain on paper towel. In roast pan, melt 1 lb. of butter, add salt, pepper, oregano, minced garlic and crushed basil. Put the back strap into the butter mixture and put in the oven for an hr. at 350 degrees. To serve, slice the meat and pour a bit of the butter sauce over it, pass the rest to pour over hot cooked rice.

MOOSE ROAST

1-4 lb. moose roast
1 c. red wine
1 pkg. dried onion soup mix

Marinate meat in wine at least 4 hrs. or overnight. Put meat in roasting bag or foil so it cannot leak. Pour wine over meat and add onion soup on top with just a bit more salt. Cook at 325 degrees for 2½ hrs. or till tender.

BREAKFAST SAUSAGE FOR 10 LBS. MEAT

Grind with med. blade 8 lbs. moose and 2 lbs. pork if on hand or all moose using sweet back fat as part to relieve dryness of all lean meat. Combine and then mix well into meat ¼ c. salt, 2 tbsp. black pepper, 2 tbsp. ground sage, 2 tsp. ground ginger. Cover well to avoid drying of meat. To serve form into small patties and fry in heavy pan until browned. Makes a good meal at any time of the day with gravy, over rice or biscuits. That's gravy made in the pan the sausages were browned in, and tasting mighty good.

BONNET PLYME MOOSE

1 shoulder roast of moose
    Marinade sauce:
        2 c. tarragon wine vinegar
        1 tsp. atkinsons
            herb mustard
        ½ tsp. white pepper
        ½ tsp. cloves
        1 tbsp. parsley
        1 tsp. grated horseradish
        2 tbsp. salt

½ c. water
¼ tsp. of each - oregano,
    thyme, rosemary
    marjoram
1 bay leaf
3 tbsp. butter
1 tbsp. onion
1 clove garlic

Bring the sauce ingredients just to boiling point and let simmer for 5 min. Pour over moose and marinate for 48 hrs. Preheat oven to about 450 degrees. Roast moose for 30 min. then reduce heat to 325 degrees.

SPICED POT ROAST

A tender, juicy roast with the subtle flavor of spices.

- 4 lb. moose rump
- 2 med. onions
- ¼ c. fat
- ¼ c. flour
- 2 c. canned tomatoes
- 1 tsp. salt
- ¼ tsp. pepper
- 1 crushed bay leaf
- 1 tbsp. pickling spice
- ¼ c. vinegar
- 2 tbsp. brown sugar

Chop onions, fry in fat until golden brown. Rub roast in flour mixed with salt and pepper. Brown roast on all sides in a heavy pan with onions, for about 15 min. Combine remaining ingredients, pour over moose. Cover the pan and cook slowly in a moderate oven or on top of the stove for 2½-3 hrs. Let the liquid simmer, add water if necessary to keep ½" in bottom of kettle. Pared carrots, peeled onions, celery and potatoes may be added ¾ hr. before the meat is finished cooking. Remove meat, strain liquid and thicken. Beaver meat is also very good cooked this way.

EASY HAMBURGER (OR MOOSEBURGER) BAKE

Season meat with salt, pepper and chopped onion. If very fat, add some fine cracker crumbs - mooseburger usually doesn't need these, though. Place in greased casserole and spread 1 tin of condensed cream of chicken or cream of mushroom soup over top. Bake ta 350 degrees F. for an hr. or more, depending on amount of meat. About half way through cooking time, stir the mixture to blend the soup well.

SAUERBRATEN — BEEF OR MOOSE

Put roast in container suitable for pickling. Pour over the following mixture, turning meat once daily to soak all over. Keep in cool place for 3-4 days.

- 1 med. onion, chopped
- ¾ c. vinegar (or red wine)
- 3-6 whole cloves
- 2 med. bay leaves
- 1 c. cold water
- 1 tbsp. sugar
- 1 tsp. salt

When ready to cook, flour meat and brown in pan - use brine for juice and cook on stove top - thicken gravy. Very nice flavour! Different! Serve with potato dumplings.

MOOSE TONGUE

1-4 lb. tongue-precooked until almost tender

2 tins tomato soup	¼ piece small hot red pepper, crumbled
1 tin water	
1 large onion (diced)	1 clove garlic
1 green pepper, diced	½ tsp. chili powder
Salt and pepper to taste	½ lb. mushrooms (optional)
1 tbsp. sugar	

Saute onion, celery, green pepper, add tomato soup and water. Add mushrooms and simmer 5 min. Peel and slice tongue, brown lightly in hot fat, then add sauce and simmer approx. 1½ hrs. Add peas 15 min. before serving. Serve with steamed rice.

STUFFED HEART

Wash heart in salt water. Pat dry. Prepare any favourite stuffing recipe. Stuff the heart and season the outside with garlic salt, black pepper, ½ tsp. oregano. Grease the heart and pan. Roast for 3 to 4 hrs. at 350 degrees.

GLAZES FOR HEART
    Apricot glaze
    Stud heart with garlic cloves
    Prepare dried apricots - 1 c. mashed
    Glaze heart an hr. before removing from oven.

    Sweet and sour sauce
    Barbecue Sauce
    Chili sauce

ROAST HEART WITH DRESSING

Wash heart thoroughly in plenty of cold water. Dry off with paper towel. Fill with dressing and put in roaster. Add 2 tbsp. lard or other shortening, salt and pepper. Cover and roast till done in med. oven, basting occasionally.

DRESSING -
      ½ loaf stale bread crumbs   1 tsp. poultry seasoning
      1 med. onion   Pinch of salt and pepper
      1 tbsp. shortening

Mix well and fill heart. Serve piping hot.

HEADCHEESE WITHOUT THE HEAD

4 pork hocks
4 deer shanks or 2 moose shanks

Cut meat from bones into very small pieces. Then put meat and bones into large pot. Cover with water. Add salt, pepper, garlic salt and onion salt. Cover. Boil slowly until well done and the meat falls from the bones. When done pour into loaf pans. Cool well. When it is set, it slices nicely, and is very good for sandwiches.

MOOSE HEAD CHEESE

Head of moose, tongue, heart and trimmings.
      ½ c. salt   1 gallon water

Clean head, removing eyes, ears, brains and skin. Trim off fat. Cut head into pieces. Soak in brine of a half c. salt to 1 gallon of water overnight. Drain and rinse in clean water. Place all in a large pot and boil meat. Trim meat from bones and chop fine. Weigh meat on kitchen scales, strain broth, then boil it down to 4 c. for every 3 lbs. of meat. Add chopped meat to broth with 1 tbsp. salt and 1 tsp. pepper, 1 tbsp. onion flakes, 1 tbsp. dried red and green pepper flakes, 1 tsp. allspice and ½ tsp. cloves for every 3 lbs. of meat. Heat mixture and simmer for 15 min. Pour into loaf pans, cover and chill.

MOOSE MEAT FONDUE

      1 coleman single burner   1 Dutch oven
      Fondue forks   Salad oil
Any type of wild game meat, cut in 1" cubes and 2 or more sauces.

Pour salad oil into Dutch oven to no more than ½ capacity. Heat oil to 425 degrees on the stove. Transfer oil to burner on the table. Set out several small bowls and 2 or more sauces. Set 2 large bowls of meat or each type of meat in an individual bowl. Each spears one or two cubes of meat then holds it in the hot oil until cooked to desired doneness then dips it in the sauce.

TYPES OF SAUCES
Curry sauce
Tomato sauce
Sweet & sour sauce
Bazil butter
Hot mustard sauce
Barbeque sauce

PEMMICAN

The best pemmican is made from the dried, powdered meat. It can be used with lard, bear fat, caribou fat, goose fat or moose fat. Smoke the dried meat. Pound it and make a nice powder. Mix like a batter. Some people like to add berries and sugar. In winter, put it outside to freeze. Keep it frozen. In the summer, make it more like a dough and cover it. It keeps well for a long time. Pemmican is used, especially in the winter, by trappers when they walk all day and want to light travel. A piece the size of a date square is enough for a meal. It is good with a cup of tea.

COUNTRY PLATE

½ lb. boneless moose
¼ lb. cooked tongue
1 tbsp. parsley
1 tsp. atkinsons herb mustard
¼ tsp. (each of thyme, cloves, cinnamon
1 small clove of garlic mashed
½ tsp. unflavored gelatin
¼ lb. raw liver
1 small onion
1 tsp. powdered ginger
Salt to taste
1/8 tsp. freshly ground black pepper

Grind the moose, tongue, liver and onion together using a fine blade of the meat grinder add the next 10 ingredients and work together with your hands. Put in a deep 2½ c. baking dish, cover and bake for 1 hr. in a preheated 350 degree oven. Keep pouring off excess grease. Dissolve gelatin in 1 tbsp. of water and spoon over. Chill for several hrs.

MEAT CAKES

This is a good way to get rid of your tougher cuts of wild game.

For 1 lb. ground meat:
1 tsp. salt
½ to 1 tsp. pepper
¼ c. catsup or tomato paste
½ to ¼ c. chopped onion

Mix all ingredients to ground meat. Shape into patties or cakes and fry in hot well greased pan.

CORNED WILD GAME

To cure a 5 lb. cut of meat (any)
- 6 tbsp. salt
- 5 tbsp. sugar brown or white
- 1 to 2 tsp. saltpeter
- 1 tbsp. pepper

Trim meat of all fat and sinew. Mix ingredients with enough water to cover meat. Let cure for 2 days. Wash several times in cold, clear water. Boil under tender. Serve with cooked cabbage. Boiled or fried with sliced onion.

MOOSE MEAT WITH ZIPPY SAUCE

- 2 tbsp. salad oil
- 1 tbsp. vinegar
- 2 tsp. chili powder
- 1 tsp. dry mustard
- 1 tsp. sugar
- 1 tsp. paprika
- 1 tsp. salt
- 1/4 tsp. pepper
- 1 small onion, chopped
- 1 clove garlic, minced
- 3 1/4 c. tomatoes
- 2 lb. minced beef

Combine all ingredients except meat in saucepan; bring to a boil. Simmer for 40 minutes. Brown minced beef, add sauce. Serve with cooked hot spaghetti.

PIT BARBEQUE

Pits should be 4 feet deep, 3 feet wide by 4 long. This will handle 25 pounds of meat which will feed approximately 50 people.

Fuel may be dry oak or poplar cord wood. Dry oak fence posts are good. 4 cords are needed for one pit. The secret of success lies in burning enough fuel to make a deep layer (2 feet) of hot coals. All unburned pieces must be removed from pit before putting the meat in on the deep bed of red hot coals. Start the fire about 20 hours before the meat is to be eaten. The meat should be placed in pit 12 hours before eating.

Sand is needed to cover the hot coals, coarse dry sand about one inch in depth. Steel bars are needed to lay across the top of the pit to support plywood or other suitable covering. This is covered with several inches of soil to seal the pit and retain steam and heat.

Meat should be hung 10 days. Red or blue grade hips are a good buy rather than a side as there is less waste. The beef (or buffalo meat) is boned and rolled in roasts and wrapped in double stockingette by packers or local butchers. The meat should not be frozen. After the fires have been started, a paste of flour and water is applied to the stockingette, and then roasts are wrapped in burlap, and tied with a wire which makes it easier to place in and take out of the pit. Roll is dipped in water before being placed in the pit allowing the heat to circulate around them.

The result...Excellent and remembered by all.

GAME OMELETTE

6 eggs
½ c. butter
Salt and pepper

½ c. chopped green onions
½ c. of remains of any cold game or bird game

Mix and fry ingredients as for ordinary omelette. In a separate pan combine meat and onion and heat. When omelette is done, spoon game mixture over top, fold and serve hot. For variation, add grated cheese.

KEBOB (LIVER) - (Venison, Elk)

Liver, cubed or sliced
Bacon strips - rolled
Mushroom caps

Cracker Crumbs
Oil

Dry liver. Alternate liver, bacon and mushrooms. Baste in oil and roll in cracker crumbs. Season with salt and pepper. Broil until tender.

KEBOB
(Venison, Elk or Moose)

2 lbs. meat, cubed
2 onions, quartered
1 dozen mushroom caps

2 tomatoes, cut in wedges
2 green peppers, cut
marinade

Soak meat cubes in marinade overnight. Place meat and vegetables alternately on skewers. Baste with marinade and broil, basting often.

SEE OUR COMPLETE LINE OF QUALITY TIRES

AAA ROAD SERVICE
CAR - BATTERIES - TUBES

286-5284

IF NO ANSWER CALL ROGER 286-5668

TOWN & COUNTRY TIRE SERVICE, INC.

HWY. 12 E.   COKATO

THE QUALITY GOES IN BEFORE THE NAME GOES ON

JIM'S TV & STEREO

DIAL
286-2132

Modular Stereo & Tape Equipment Radios

Color & B/W TV's
*Service All Makes
No Milage Fee*

135 3RD ST E   COKATO

RT. 2, BOX 93
COKATO, MN. 55321

*Write for free
fun schedule*

A FAMILY
CAMPGROUND WITH

• Ponies • Pools • Fishing
• Cottages • Mini Golf
• Tennis Courts
• Saturday Evening Entertainment
• Rental Boats • Bait
• Groceries

(612) 286-5779

TOM THUMB

COMPLETE LINE OF QUALITY GROCERIES
DELICATESSEN
FRESH FRUITS & VEGETABLES
FRESH DONUTS - DAILY

Open 7 Days a Week, 6:00 a.m. - 11:00 p.m.

SELF-SERVICE GASOLINE

305 Cokato St. W.   **286-5631**   Cokato

COLE'S
AUTO BODY

Alvin Cole, Owner

Cokato, Minn.
Phone: 286-2416

DR. AUDREE L. PALMQUIST
CHIROPRACTOR
DR. TIMOTHY C. PALMQUIST
CHIROPRACTOR

270 MILLARD AVE., P.O. BOX 299, COKATO, MN 55321
BUS. 612/286-5893   RES. 612/286-5263

the Saloon

Homemade Pizza To Go

Phone 286-5909
COKATO, MN.

LUNDEEN FURNITURE, INC.

- Furniture
- Reupholstering
- Floor Covering
- Ceramic

"Quality and Service"
Cash and carry for lowest prices.
RALPH LUNDEEN

370 Millard Ave.   Cokato, Mn.   286-2611

BRAISED BEAR

Marinate bear steak overnight. Dry and sear on both sides in hot cooking oil or bacon grease. Add the following:

    ½ tsp. garlic salt   dash of pepper
    ½ tsp. onion salt   ½ tsp. chili powder

Cover and simmer for 2 to 3 hours, until tender. Add:

    4 sliced onions   2 cans tomato soup

Simmer 15 to 20 minutes more. If you wish to thicken juice for gravy, add flour.

BEAR STEAK

Marinate steak for 24 hours; wipe dry

Sauce:
    4 sliced onions   3 tbsp. chives
    3 tbsp. butter   1 tsp. prepared mustard
    1 c. water   2 tbsp. tomato paste
    Salt & pepper to taste   1 dash of Worcestershire
    1 clove garlic, crushed   sauce

Saute onions in water and butter. Season with salt and pepper. Add remaining ingredients and simmer a few minutes. Broil steak to desired doneness. Put on platter and pour sauce over steak. Add buttered sauteed mushrooms.

BARBECUED BEAR

    1 2-3 lb. bear roast   1/8 tsp. cayenne pepper
    Salt and pepper   2 tbsp. Worcestershire sauce
    1 clove of garlic   ¼ c. vinegar
    2 tbsp. brown sugar   1 c. tomato juice
    1 tbsp. paprika   ¼ c. catsup
    1 tsp. dry mustard   ½ c. water
    ¼ tsp. chili powder

Place roast in small roaster. Season with salt, pepper and garlic. Roast at 350 degrees for 1 hr. or until well done. Slice into thin slices. Mix 1 tsp. salt with remaining ingredients in heavy skillet. Simmer for 15 mins. Add meat; simmer for 1 hr. or until meat is tender. Yield: 6-8 servings.

CAMP SIZE BEAR STEW

8 lbs. bear meat
Carrots
Onions
1 celery stalk

1½ oz. vinegar
2 lbs. mushrooms
Garlic salt; salt and
    pepper to taste

Cut off fat from bear meat, slice into large pieces and brown. Cube all the vegetables and simmer meat with half of the carrot, onion and all of the celery. Add the vinegar when meat and vegetables are cooked. Remove carrots, celery and onions and discard. Put in the remaining half of carrots, onions and simmer again. Cook until nearly done then add mushrooms. Thicken stew as you would gravy. Season with salt and pepper and garlic salt to taste.

MUSKRAT MEAT LOAF

1 muskrat
1/8 c. dry crumbs
    (bread or crackers)
¼ tsp. thyme
¼ tsp. pepper

2 eggs, beaten
1 c. evaporated milk
¼ onion, minced or grated
1 tsp. salt
1 tsp. Worcestershire sauce

Soak muskrat overnight in salted solution (1 tbsp. salt to 1 qt. water). Remove meat from bones and grind. Mix ground meat thoroughly with other ingredients. Place in meat loaf dish. Place dish in pan containing hot water. Bake in oven, 350 degrees for 1½ to 2 hrs. Serves six.

MUSKRAT

1 muskrat per person
onion, cut
1 carrot

1 stalk celery
Salt and pepper

Wash and clean muskrat completely. All fat and musk must be removed. Parboil with onion, carrot and celery. Bring to a boil. Cook for 20 minutes; let stand with the cover on for 20 minutes. Drain well. Do not use broth. Brown muskrat in oil in a skillet until brown using seasoning. (Musk is found between the shoulders, underneath the arms, on the back, back quarters by the tail, and under back legs.)

BEAVER, MUSKRAT, PORCUPINE, RABBIT, COON

Flour
Paprika
Salt and pepper
Onion, sliced

Garlic salt
½ inch of water in bottom
  of roaster so it doesn't
  cook dry

Be sure animal is completely defated. Soak in salt water overnight. Drain, and soak in fresh water until ready to use. Dry off. Cut meat into serving pieces. Place pieces in a brown paper bag containing flour mixture. Fry until golden brown. Place in a roaster. Add rest of the ingredients. Oven temperature 375-400 degrees for 2 hours.

SWEET PICKLED BEAVER

1 beaver, skinned & cleaned
½ c. vinegar
1 tbsp. salt
2 tsp. soda
½ c. dry white wine
  or apple juice

1 tsp. cinnamon
½ tsp. cloves
½ c. brown sugar
2 tbsp. dry mustard
1 c. pineapple juice
Juice & grated rind
  of 1 lemon

1) Wash beaver thoroughly with salt water, then let soak overnight in enough cold water to cover, adding ½ c. vinegar and 1 tbsp. salt to the water.
2) The next day, remove the beaver from the brine, wash and cover with a solution of 2 qts. of water to 2 tsp. soda. Birng to a boil, reduce heat and simmer 10 min.
3) Drain and rinse the beaver then place it in a clean pot. Add water just to cover. Sprinkle mixed pickling spice on top, bring to a boil, reduce heat and simmer 20 min.
4) Drain and rinse beaver. Pat dry and place in roaster.
5) Mix mustard, spices, sugar, wine and fruit juices and spread over beaver.
6) Cover and roast at 325 degrees until tender, basting frequently.

MAKING BEAVER STEW ... IN THE BUSH

Skin and clean the beaver
Remove the head and feet
Cut meat into small pieces
Cut pieces in the pot

Add water, salt and pepper. Cover.
Boil meat until tender.

Cooking time will depend on the size of beaver. A large animal, using all the meat, about 4 hours.

BEAVER TAIL BEANS

Blister tail over fire till skin loosens or dip in boiling water for a couple of minutes. Pull skin off. Cut up and boil with a pot of beans. Add salt and pepper to taste. Some chopped onions adds to the flavour. Beaver tail is also good roasted over a campfire or in the oven.

BEAVER BURGERS

Beaver meat	Salt
Onions	Pepper
Cooking oil	Oleo

Grind up fresh beaver meat; with onions to taste. Fry in medium hot pan as you would hamburgers. Salt and pepper. Add small amount of oleo to fry in. Just enough to keep from sticking.

BEAVER MEAT LOAF

Sage   Favorite Meat-loaf recipe

Make any meat loaf you like and substitute beaver for beef. A large pinch of sage adds to the taste.

BEAVER TAIL

This tid-bit of the old-time trappers will be tasted by few of our generation, more's the pity. Broil over hot coals for a few minutes. The rough, scaly hide will blister and come off, leaving the tail clean, white and solid. Then roast or boil until tender. This is considered very strengthening food. (use only young beaver). For a treat, cool, souse in vinegar, add raw onion rings and salt and pepper to taste.

BEAVER

Strips of bacon or salt pork
1 c. chopped carrots
1 c. chopped celery
Dash of poultry dressing

1-2 c. water
1 c. chopped onion
Salt and pepper to taste

Use only young beaver. Remove head, skin and excess fat. Rinse well. Put in roaster and cut slits on back and sides. Lay strips of bacon or salt pork on top so grease may penetrate into slits. Add vegetables, spices and water adding more water as needed. Cook till tender. OR Same as above, only make a stuffing as for turkey or chicken, using garlic salt, pepper and onions. Eliminate vegetables.

POSSUM & CHESTNUTS

Salt and pepper
Chestnuts
Applesauce
Butter

Bread crumbs
Sweet potato
Lemon juice

Skin the possum and remove the glands and entrails. Scrape clean and scald in boiling water. Rub inside and out with salt and pepper and set in cool place. Stuff with chestnuts, applesauce and bread crumbs in equal proportions. Cover with slices of sweet potato, 1 c. boiling water, ½ c. lemon juice. Bake in butter and baste often until tender.

GROUND HOG

1/8 tsp. celery salt
1/8 tsp. pleasoning seasoning
¼ tsp. minced onion
1/8 tsp. mill-ground black pepper
Your favorite barbecue sauce

Skin chuck and soak in strong salt water, for about 4 hrs. Next, cut up as you would a rabbit. Immerse in boiling water (15 mins. per lb.). The water should have just a bit of celery salt and minced onion and mill-ground black pepper. When meat is tender, remove from water and dry with paper towels. Cook on charcoal grill after basting with your favorite barbecue sauce. Turn over as each piece is browned to your liking. Test with fork to be sure all meat is thoroughly cooked. (Check the game laws, because in some states ground hogs are illegal.)

POT ROAST WOODCHUCK

½ tsp. salt
½ tsp. pepper
1 c. boiling water
¼ to ½ c. flour

Clean and wash chuck. Cut in small pieces. Soak 2 hours in cold salted water. Dry. Season with salt and pepper and roll in flour. Fry in hot bacon grease until brown. Add 1 c. boiling water, cover and cook slow. (About 4 hours). Add more water if needed. When done thicken juice with flour.

ANTELOPE (STEAKS OR CHOP)

6-8 steaks or chops
1-2 c. cracker crumbs
Salt and pepper
¼ tsp. garlic salt
½ pkg. onion soup mix

Wash meat. Roll in cracker crumbs. Sesaon with salt, pepper and garlic salt. Place in greased cooking pan or baking sheet. Sprinkle with onion soup mix. Bake at 375 to 400 degrees for 30 to 45 minutes, or until tender.

PORCUPINE

He is better than he looks. Parboil 30 minutes and roast or broil him to a golden brown. Season to taste. He will need no pork to make him juicy, you will find him like a spring lamb, only better. One part of the porcupine is a delicacy - the liver, it may be fried with bacon, or baked slowly.

TRICASSEED SQUIRREL

1 squirrel (cut into serving pieces)
1/8 tsp. pepper
½ c. flour
3 slices of bacon, chopped
1 tsp. salt
1 tbsp. dehydrated onions or 1 medium dry onion
2 tsp. lemon juice
⅓ c. water

Wash and clean the squirrel. Rub pieces with salt and pepper and roll in flour. Pan fry with chopped bacon for 30 minutes, over moderate heat. Add onions and lemon juice and water. Cover tightly and cook slowly for about 4½ hours.

FRIED SQUIRREL

1 squirrel
Salted water
Flour
Cooking oil

Dress squirrel. Wash thoroughly. Cut in pieces for serving. Cover with salted water; let stand overnight. Drain. Roll in flour. If not tender, parboil 10 minutes, drain. Fry in cooking fat until tender. If squirrel is young, parboiling is not necessary.

ROAST SQUIRRELS

3 small squirrels
¾ c. cooking oil
¼ c. lemon juice
2 c. bread crumbs
½ c. milk or cream
1 c. sliced mushrooms sauted
½ tsp. salt
1/8 tsp. pepper
½ tsp. onion juice
4 tbsp. olive oil or bacon fat

Dress and clean squirrels, wash and dry. Cover with cooking oil mixed with lemon juice and let stand for 1 hour. Combine crumbs with just enough milk to moisten mushrooms, salt, pepper and onion juice. Stuff squirrels with this mixture, sew and truss. Place in roaster. Brush with olive oil or bacon fat. Roast uncovered in slow oven 325 degrees until tender 1½ to 1¾ hours. Baste every 15 minutes with fat. Serve with pan gravy.

SQUIRREL STEW

2 squirrels, medium or large
3 quarts water
3 medium potatoes
2 raw onions
3 to 4 carrots
2 tsp. salt
1 tsp. pepper

Clean, wash and cut squirrel into small pieces. Put in pot, add cold water and bring to a boil. Simmer until tender. Add vegetables and seasonings. Cook until meat falls from bones.

DEEP FRIED SQUIRREL

Dressed squirrel
2 egg yolks
4 tbsp. cracker crumbs
Fat for frying

Cut squirrel in four portions. Drop pieces in boiling water and boil 15 mins. Remove pieces and dry on towel. Prepare batter of egg yolks and cracker crumbs. Dip meat in batter and deep fry in smoking hot fat (375 degrees F.).

SQUIRREL AND GRAVY

1 squirrel, cut up
Water
2 tbsp. flour
1/8 tsp. salt
Dash of pepper

Place squirrel in a 1½ qt. cooker. Cover with water; cook over low heat for 1 hr. and 30 mins. or until tender. Remove squirrel; drain off all but 2 tbsp. drippings. Stir in flour, salt and pepper. Add 1 c. water or milk; place squirrel in gravy and heat. Yield: 8 servings.

SQUIRREL

3 dressed squirrels
Flour
Salt and pepper
1 c. water

Quarter the squirrels and roll in flour and pan fry as one would a chicken. Salt and pepper to taste. When brown on both sides, add water and simmer on top of stove for 1 hr. or until tender. Make your favorite gravy. Serves 6.

FROG LEGS

Frogs
Salt
Pepper
1 egg, slightly beaten
Fine bread crumbs
Cooking oil

Slip skin off hind quarters of frogs. Wash frog legs thoroughly. Dry. Rub with salt and pepper. Dip in slightly beaten egg. Roll in fine bread crumbs. Fry in deep fat (385 degrees F.) until well browned.

BREADED FROG LEGS

Frog legs (hind quarters only) are quite delicious. The skin can be turned over and skinned off like a glove.

>6 frog legs, skinned
>1 egg
>Lemon juice
>Salt and pepper
>Fine bread crumbs

Wash legs in cold water; dry well on a towel. Season with salt, pepper and lemon juice. Dip in beaten egg, then in fine bread crumbs. Serve with tartar sauce.

RACCOON

Skin and dress. Remove scent glands from under each front leg and on either side of spine. Wash in cold water. Parboil in 1 or 2 waters, depending upon the age. Stuff with dressing (like a chicken). Bake to a delicate brown.

RACCOON PIE

>1 raccoon
>1 qt. water
>1 pt. vinegar
>1 tbsp. salt
>1 tsp. pepper
>1 tbsp. brown sugar
>¼ oz. pickling spices
>1 onion, diced
>4 small potatoes
>4 small carrots

Gravy:
>2 c. broth
>2 tbsp. butter
>5 tbsp. browned flour
>1 recipe baking
>   powder biscuits

Cut prepared raccoon in serving pieces. Mix water, seasonings, sugar and spices together. Put raccoon pieces in this brine about 8 hrs. or more. Drain; put in stewing kettle and cover with water. Cook until meat is tender. Add onion, potatoes and carrots. When all ingredients are tender, remove from broth. Thicken liquid with browned flour and butter and season to taste. Place meat and vegetables in a dish and cover with gravy. Cover the top with your own recipe for baking powder biscuits, with a little extra shortening in dough. Bake in 450 degree oven until brown, about 12 to 15 mins. Serves 8.

ROASTED RACCOON WITH GRAVY

1 raccoon, cleaned
Beef suet
3 stalks celery, chopped
1 large onion, chopped
1 tsp. seasoned salt
  (onion blend)
¼ tsp. pepper
1 c. hot water

Cut prepared raccoon into serving pieces (cut off all fat.) Render beef suet in skillet and brown pieces. Place in roaster pan and add celery and onions. Sprinkle with seasoned salt and pepper. Add 1 c. hot water. Roast in 350 degree oven about 2½ to 3 hrs. Gravy can be made from drippings or stock. Use 2½ c. liquid, 3 tbsp. flour and 2 beef bouillon cubes. Dissolve cubes in a small amount of water. Simmer until thickens.

BARBECUE FOR VENISON RIBS OR COON

Large bottle catsup
1 c. water
1 tsp. chili powder
1 tsp. Worcestershire sauce
1 tsp. Heinz 57 sauce
¼ c. vinegar
Salt and pepper
2 or 3 drops tabasco sauce

Brown meat. Mix and pour over meat. Bake at 350 degrees until tender. Slice onions, if desired.

TO PREPARE A TURTLE

First cut off the head and feet and turn it upside down nailing the tail to a board. Use a very sharp thin knife and cut the skin from around the back. Cut off the belly plate; skin the neck and tail and other skin off. Remove the internal organs. Also remove the 2 tenderloin strips along the back. Cut the fatty tissue away and wash the turtle meat in cold water and you are ready to cook it. It has a taste almost like chicken.

MOSS BACK TURTLE

Cut the head off; turn upside down so it will bleed well, almost an hr. Skin; remove the flesh from the shell. Cut meat in medium pieces; soak in salt water, 1 c. to a gallon of water, about an hr. Season with salt and pepper. Fry in hot lard until brown and well done. Turn often. Serve with hot baking biscuits, mashed potatoes and apple pie.

COKATO HARDWARE

Jerry Gilmer, Owner

COKATO, MINN. 55321
Phone 286-2513

MORE THAN A HARDWARE STORE

LUNDEEN IMPLEMENT

Dealer In Used Farm
& Industrial Equipment
Cars, Trucks, & Pickups

Cokato, Minn. Ph. 612-286-2156
Denny *Jerry*

BOB'S ROOFING & CONSTRUCTION
WESSMAN OIL CO.
COKATO MOTOR SALES, INC.
MONTGOMERY WARD
MR. K's CAFE

Tell Our Advertisers You Have Read Their Advertisement In This Book

COKATO HARDWARE

Jerry Gilmer, Owner

COKATO, MINN. 55321
Phone 286-2513

MORE THAN A HARDWARE STORE

OUR OWN

LUNDEEN IMPLEMENT

Dealer in Used Farm
& Industrial Equipment
Cars, Trucks, & Pickups

Ph. 612 286-2158   Cokato, Minn.
Jerry   Denny

BOB'S ROOFING & CONSTRUCTION
WISSMAN OIL CO.
COKATO MOTOR SALES, INC.
MONTGOMERY WARD
MR. K's CAFE

Tell Our Advertisers
You Have Read
Their Advertisement
In This Book

TURTLE PIE

1½ c. turtle meat
    cut in cubes
3 tbsp. flour

1 onion, diced
3 tbsp. butter
1½ c. water

Brown the turtle meat in butter; add diced onion and salt and pepper to taste. Add the water and let simmer for about an hr., then remove it from the water and put in a greased casserole. Make a thin flour paste and add it to the turtle meat. Make a baking powder biscuit dough and cover the casserole with it. Bake in hot oven until the biscuits are brown.

TURTLE STEW

2¼ c. turtle meat
    cut in 1" cubes
2 c. diced celery
3 med. carrots,
    peeled & diced
1 c. tomatoes
Salt and pepper

4 tbsp. margarine
1 med. onion, sliced
3 med. potatoes, peeled
    and diced
1 c. fresh lima beans
½ c. parsley

Place onion, lima beans, celery in Dutch oven and cover with water. Bring to boil and simmer 30 mins. In meantime, saute the turtle meat in margarine in skillet until brown on all sides. Add meat, margarine, potatoes, carrots, tomatoes, parsley, salt and pepper to the vegetables in Dutch oven. Simmer for 45 mins. or until all vegetables are tender. Serves 6.

TURTLE STEAKS

Slice turtle meat in slices; dip in flour and fry in hot fat as you would fry round steak or chicken.

FRIED TURTLE

1 med. sized turtle
1 tsp. salt
½ tsp. pepper

2 bay leaves
Seasoned flour
Fat or butter

Clean and disjoint the turtle into medium-sized pieces. Place in a stewing kettle with salt, pepper and bay leaves. Add water to cover meat and boil for 15 mins. Let turtle cool in its broth. Drain well. Dust with seasoned flour and fry in a heavy skillet, as you would chicken, until it is tender and golden brown. If you wish, make a cream gravy from the residue in the skillet.

TURTLE

A turtle
Flour
Season to taste
Water
Cooking oil

Remove from shell, dress and wash thoroughly. Cut into serving pieces. Roll in flour and brown in cooking fat. When browned, add enough water to cover bottom of pan, season. Cover and cook until tender. Add water as needed to keep from burning.

RABBIT STEW

Clean and skin the rabbit. When skinning,
1) Start at the ankle
2) Run the point of the knife around the ankle
3) Pull the skin off up to the shoulder
4) Cut off the right legs
5) Cut off the ears
6) Pull the skin off shoulder and head. Cut meat into parts including the bones. Put meat in pot, add water to cover. Now add these:

2 c. flour
4 tbsp. lard
1 tsp. baking powder
½ tsp. salt

Make a dough of this, break and add to top of the stew in pieces.

RABBIT STEW

2 rabbits
Onion
Salt and pepper
6 carrots
Pinch of sweet basil
3 stalks celery

Stew:

potatoes
Flour

Dumplings
Clean rabbit. Parboil in water. Season with onions, carrots, basil and celery, salt and pepper. For stew: potatoes boiled until soft. Thicken with flour mixture. With dumplings: Baking powder dumplings; thicken broth with 1 c. flour.

HASENPFEFFER

Place cut up rabbit in a crock jar and cover with vinegar and water (equal parts). Add 1 sliced onion, salt and pepper to taste, cloves and 2 bay leaves. Allow to soak for 2 days. Remove meat and brown thoroughly in hot butter, turning it often and gradually add the sauce in which it was pickled. Simmer ½ hr. or until tender. Before serving, add 1 c. thick sour cream. The amount of water and vinegar depends on the amount of meat pieces. (Equal amounts of water and vinegar to cover meat).

RABBIT FOR TWO

1 rabbit, deboned and unmarinated
    ½ peeled & pitted lemon
    4 tbsp. water
    4 pork sausages
    4 tbsp. bread crumbs
    1 tsp. Worcestershire
        sauce
    1½ tbsp. vinegar
    1 tbsp. water

1 pkg. Lipton onion
    soup (dry)
1 med. raw potato
1 tbsp. margarine
2 shakes of black pepper
1½ tsp. sugar
1 tbsp. cornstarch

Debone one rabbit and cut into ½" cubes. In a separate pot boil the pork sausage for 15 mins. Remove; let cool and cut into ½" lengths. Dice 1 potato and set aside with rabbit and pork. Melt the margarine in a skillet under very low heat. Add dry onion soup, finely chopped lemon and 4 tbsp. water. Stir; simmer for 5 mins. In a cup, mix cornstarch, 1 tbsp. water, vinegar, Worcestershire sauce, sugar and pepper. Set aside. Place rabbit in the pan and brown for 5 mins. Then add pork, potatoes, and cornstarch sauce. Cover and simmer over medium heat for 45 mins. For the crowning touch, uncover; jack up the heat to high. Add bread crumbs; stir gently and cook for 5 mins. Works fine with squirrels and venison, also.

FRIED RABBIT

Dressed rabbit, cut into pieces
    1 c. flour
    1 tsp. salt
    ¼ tsp. pepper
    2 tbsp. salad oil

1 tbsp. butter
1 chicken bouillon cube
½ c. hot water

Dredge rabbit pieces in seasoned flour until well-coated. Brown on all sides in the salad oil and butter in skillet. Dissolve bouillon in the hot water and pour over the meat. Cover and cook for 45 mins. over low heat.

BARBECUED WILD RABBIT

1 lge. onion, minced
1 clove of garlic, minced
2 green peppers, minced
1 can tomato juice
1 c. water
1 c. vinegar
½ c. catsup

½ c. Worcestershire sauce
¼ c. butter
1 tsp. salt
½ tsp. cayenne or red
    pepper pods
2 or 3 rabbits, cut up

Combine all ingredients except rabbits; boil for 5 to 10 mins. Place rabbit pieces in pan in single layer. Pour sauce over rabbit, covering completely. Bake at 250 degrees for 3 hrs. or until tender, turning occasionally. Yield: 6-8 servings.

RABBIT STEW

1, 2½-3 lb. rabbit
1 bay leaf
½ lb. sliced fresh
    mushrooms
1/8 tsp. pepper
2 qts. boiling water
2 c. diced pared carrots
2 c. diced pared potatoes

6 small white onions, peeled
1½ c. diced celery
4½ tsp. salt
½ c. flour
¾ c. cold water
1 tbsp. chopped parsley
Dash tabasco sauce

Order rabbit drawn, cleaned and cut up. Wash and place in a kettle with the onions, bay leaf, celery, salt, pepper and boiling water. Cover; bring to a boil and simmer for 2 hrs. or until rabbit is nearly tender. Then add carrots, potatoes and mushrooms. Cover and simmer for 30 mins. longer or until vegetables and rabbit are tender. Blend flour with the cold water and stir into the gently boiling stew. Cook until thickened. Add parsley and tabasco and serve. Serves 6-8.

RABBIT SMOTHERED WITH ONIONS

3 lge. onions, sliced
3 tbsp. shortening
1 3-lb. rabbit, cut up
Flour
1 c. sour cream
Salt and pepper to taste

Fry onions in shortening in a skillet; remove from skillet. Dredge rabbit in flour. Saute rabbit in remaining shortening in skillet until brown on both sides. Cover with onions; pour sour cream over the top. Cover; cook slowly for 1 hr. on top of stove or bake at 350 degrees for 35 to 45 mins. Uncover; bake for 15 mins. longer. Season with salt and pepper.

RABBIT IN RHINE WINE SAUCE

Cut up rabbits in serving pieces. Shake well with flour and brown well in butter. Pour 1 or 2 jiggers of 100 proof whiskey over rabbit and set aflame. Remove rabbits and make a sauce of (depending on how many rabbits):
 1 bottle of Rhine wine
 4 cans chicken broth
Thicken with flour. When thick, add:
 3 bay leaves
 1 c. stuffed olives
 1 small jar cocktail onions and juice
 A small can of mushroom pieces and juice may be added
Place meat back in gravy and bake until done. The amount of gravy depends on the number of meat pieces; be sure the meat is thoroughly covered with gravy. Crisp fried bacon pieces may be served on top, if desired.

BAKED RABBIT

2-2 lb. rabbits, cut up
2 tsp. salt
1/8 tsp. pepper
¼ c. sliced onions
¼ c. & 2 tbsp. flour
¼ c. fat or salad oil
2 bouillon cubes
2¼ c. boiling water

Wash and dry the cleaned, cut up rabbits. Roll in ¼ c. flour combined with salt and the pepper. Cook the sliced onions until tender in the fat in a Dutch oven or skillet. Remove the onions and brown the rabbit in the same fat. Place the onions and the bouillon cubes, which have been dissolved in 2 c. boiling water, over the rabbit. Cover; bake in a moderate 350 degree F. oven for 1½ hrs. or until tender. Stir into the gravy the remaining 2 tbsp. flour mixed with the remaining ¼ c. water. Serves 5-6.

RABBIT GLISONCE

Celery	Onion
Salt pork	

Glisonce:

2 c. flour	1 tsp. salt
Egg	Water

Clean and wash rabbit. Cut into serving pieces. Boil rabbit for a broth. Add celery, onion and salt pork. Boil for 2 hours. Remove rabbit.
Glisonce: Combine flour, salt, egg and enough dough to make a pie crust consistancy dough. Flour a board; roll out very thin; cut into wide strips and drop in boiling water. Steam for 20 minutes at medium heat. Serve over rabbit.

RABBIT CACCIATORA

2 rabbits, serving pieces	
Green pepper	1 pkg. spaghetti mix
Mushrooms	2 tbsp. oil

Brown rabbit in oil. Make up spaghetti mix. Pour over rabbit. In electric skillet, fry at 225 degrees for 30 minutes. (Tastes great with rice).

ROAST RABBIT

1 rabbit	Sage stuffing
Salt and pepper	2 tbsp. fat

Wash dressed rabbit thoroughly under running water. Dry. Sprinkle salt and pepper on inside. Fill with stuffing, fasten opening securely and spread with fat. Sprinkle with salt and pepper and roast in uncovered pan 325 degrees F. Roast 1½ to 1-¾ hours or until tender.

RABBIT FRICASSEE

2 rabbits
1 chopped onion
½ tsp. pepper
Dash of nutmeg
Dash of mace
2 c. rabbit stock

1 c. cream or milk
2 eggs, beaten
1 tbsp. butter
Flour
Juice of 1 lemon

Other seasonings may be added to suit your own taste.

Clean and wash rabbit in cold water. Cut and soak in salted water for 1 hour. Drain and cover with fresh water. Add onion and spices. Cover and simmer 1 hour. Remove meat and place in oven to keep warm. Add beaten eggs and butter to the 2 c. of rabbit stock. Thicken with flour mixed in a little milk. Bring to a boil and remove from heat. Add lemon juice, stirring constantly and pour over meat.

HASSENPFEFFER
(Sweet and Sour Rabbit)

1 rabbit
1 quart vinegar
2 tbsp. salt
1 tbsp. pickling spices
1 tbsp. peppercorns
2 large onions, sliced

2 tbsp. fat
2 tbsp. flour
1 c. cold water
1 tsp. cinnamon
½ tsp. allspice

Cut rabbit into serving portions, place in crock and cover with vinegar combined with salt, spices, peppercorns and 1 onion. Let stand in a cool place 24 hours. Drain, cover with boiling water and simmer until tender about 1½ hours. Remove meat and strain broth. Melt fat in a frying pan, blend in flour and add water, stirring constantly. Cook until thickened. Add rabbit, strained broth, cinnamon, allspice and remaining onion and simmer for 1 hour.

RABBIT STEW

2-3 lb. rabbits, cut up
3 tsp. salt
¼ tsp. pepper
flour
3 slices bacon, cut in pieces
4 onions, sliced
3 tbsp. shortening

1 clove garlic, crushed
3 c. water
¼ tsp. marjoram
4 potatoes, diced
1½ c. diced carrots
1 tsp. paprika
1 c. sour cream

Dredge the pieces of rabbit in flour seasoned with 1 tsp. salt and 1/8 tsp. pepper. Fry the bacon until crisp. Remove bacon and drain on paper towelling. Add the shortening to the bacon drippings and saute the rabbit until nicely browned. Add the onions, garlic and water. Season with marjoram, 2 tsp. salt and 1/8 tsp. pepper. Cover and simmer until tender. Add the potatoes, carrots, bacon and a little additional water. Cook until vegetables are tender. Add paprika and sour cream. Reheat but do not allow stew to boil after adding sour cream.

RABBIT PIE

¼ c. margarine
¼ c. chopped onion
¼ c. sifted flour
3½ c. coarsely cut cooked rabbit meat
salt & pepper to taste

½ c. chopped green pepper
½ tsp. accent
2½ c. rabbit broth (or water with 4 chicken bouillon cubes)
Pastry (basis) (1 c. flour)

Heat margarine in a large fry pan. Add onion and green pepper and cook about 5 minutes over low heat. Blend in the flour and cook until the mixture bubbles. Pour in the broth gradually, stirring constantly. Cook until thick and smooth, stirring frequently. Add salt and pepper, and accent. Add meat to the sauce and heat thoroughly. Pour mixture into a shallow baking dish or pan, roll out the pastry and cut slits for steam to escape. Fit to top of dish or pan, crimping the edges of the crust. Bake the pie in hot oven 425 degrees for 15-20 minutes, or until crust browns and sauce bubbles. Serves 4 to 6.

Variations: Use 1 c. of cooked diced vegetables (potatoes, carrots, celery) 2 c. of rabbit meat. Make the topping of tiny baking powder biscuits.

SMOTHERED RABBIT

⅓ c. diced strip bacon or salt pork
1 can condensed chicken broth

1-2½ lb. rabbit
1 c. light cream

Cook slowly bacon or salt pork until pieces are crisp. Rinse and pat dry 1 fresh cut-up rabbit. Add to pan. Cook covered on high heat, 20-25 minutes on each side. Rabbit should be brown and tender. Remove meat and keep warm. Add 1 can condensed chicken broth to pan. Stir. Boil fast uncovered for 5 minutes. Add 1 c. light cream. Simmer 2-3 minutes. Heat rabbit in sauce for 5 minutes. Makes 3-4 servings.

HOW TO COOK A SKUNK

Don't laugh! During the depression in the 1930's, rugged individualists who were too proud to accept welfare ate everything they could shoot or trap. They discovered, like their forefathers had done before them, that skunk meat was white, tender and tasty. It was also a favorite delicacy of the Indians. So don't knock it until you've tried it.

ROAST SKUNK

    1 c. clear soup (bouillon cube)
    2 sliced carrots
    1 tsp. onion juice

Dissolve 1 bouillon cube in 1 c. hot water. Skin, clean and remove insides. Remove scent glands. Parboil in salted water for 15 mins. Drain off water. Then place meat in fresh water and steam until tender, about 1 hr. Transfer to roasting pan and put in oven at 375 degrees.

Add 1 c. of clear soup (bouillon cube), 2 sliced carrots and 1 tsp. of onion juice and cooked uncovered for 2 hrs.

BROILED SKUNK

    Salt and pepper
    1 tsp. onion juice
    Butter

Parboil in heavily salted water for 15 mins. (Don't forget to remove the scent glands.) The pour off water and add fresh water. Steam for 1 hr. Rub with salt, pepper and onion juice and brush with butter. Broil about 40 mins. and baste every 10 mins. with butter.

CARIBOU STEW

Bacon	2 cans mushroom soup
2 med. onions	Potatoes
Celery	Carrots
5 lbs. caribou stew meat	Rutabaga
2 tbsp. flour	

Cut bacon and dice onions, green pepper and celery and put in Dutch oven with cooking oil and brown. Add caribou stew meat and brown. Add salt, pepper, garlic, season salt. After meat is browned, add water and cook. Later add vegetables. When nearly done, add 2 tins of mushroom soup and water. Let simmer and add flour to thicken.

CARIBOU STEAKS SUPREME

2 lrg. sirloin caribou steaks
Salt & pepper to taste
1 garlic clove
Garlic salt
3 green onions (chopped)

2 med. tomatoes cut in squares
½ med. green pepper (chopped)
1 c. sliced mushrooms

Season steaks with salt, pepper and garlic salt. Put in hot pan containing a little fat and fry to desired degree of doneness. Meanwhile, melt some butter in another pan, add onions, and garlic clove. After a couple of minutes add mushrooms, green pepper and tomatoes. Cook until tomatoes soften. Serve steaks covered with vegetables.

WOLF STROGANOFF

2 tbsp. butter or margarine
1 large onion, thinly sliced
1 can condensed mushroom soup

¾ c. sour cream
1 lb. good wolf rump (or other good wild meat)

Brown meat and onions in butter in a large skillet stirring occasionally. Remove from heat and stir in the soup, sour cream and water. Stir well to avoid sticking. Cover and simmer over low heat for about 1 hr., stirring occasionally. Serve over cooked egg noodles.

Wild Birds

WILD BIRDS

WILD GAME DRESSING

1 c. raisins
1 c. chopped celery
1 c. chopped onion
1 c. unsalted pecans
4 c. soft bread crumbs
1½ tsp. salt
2 eggs, well beaten
½ c. scalded milk

Put ingredients together and pour milk over mixture. Toss lightly with a fork. Use with your favorite game.

ROAST MALLARD DUCK

1 mallard duck, 1½ lbs. drawn weight
1½ tsp. salt
1/8 tsp. pepper
½ pared cored apple
1 small peeled onion
2 thin slices salt pork

Wash duck and wipe dry. Sprinkle body cavity with ½ tsp. of the salt. Sprinkle remainder of the salt and the pepper on the outside of body. Place apple and onion in the body cavity. Truss bird and place on a rack in an uncovered baking pan or roaster. Lay the slices of salt pork over the breast. Place bird in a very hot oven of 500 degrees F. and roast for 15-20 mins. if liked rare. If preferred well done, roast for 30 mins. (on basis of 20 mins. per lb.) Serves 2. Gravy may be made from the drippings in the pan, if desired. Duck may be stuffed with Wild Rice Stuffing, if preferred.

BAKED PHEASANT

Shake pheasant pieces in flour and brown in butter. Place in baking pan and pour over it:

1 can frozen orange juice mixed with
¼ c. brown sugar
¼ tsp. ginger.

Season with salt and pepper. Bake until tender.

BAKED PRAIRIE CHICKEN

1 prairie chicken
¼ c. flour
½ tsp. salt
¼ tsp. pepper

½ tsp. savory
Dash of thyme and basil
Slice bacon
¼ c. butter

Dredge bird with flour, salt, pepper and savory. Sprinkle thyme and basil on strip of bacon; roll up and fasten with toothpicks. Place bacon roll in body cavity and close the opening. Brown bird in melted butter in skillet. Transfer to baking dish. Cover and bake in 325 degree oven for 60 mins. or until tender. Make gravy with milk or light cream, if desired.

FRIED PRAIRIE CHICKEN

1 young prairie chicken
Salt and pepper

Flour
4 tbsp. fat

Clean prairie chicken; dress and cut into serving portions. Plunge into cold water; drain thoroughly, but do not wipe dry. Season well with salt and pepper and dredge with flour. Cook chicken slowly in hot fat. When chicken is brown and tender, about 1 hr.; remove to a hot platter.
Make cream gravy and serve with the prairie chicken.

BAKED PIGEON WITH MUSHROOM SOUP

Dressed pigeons
Salt and pepper

Melted butter
1 can mushroom soup

Split down the back and flatten breast. Wipe with a damp cloth inside and out. Season with salt and pepper. Put in a covered baking dish. Bake 1 hr., basting with melted butter. When done, heat 1 can mushroom soup and pour over. Bake ½ hr. or more and serve.

WILD RICE STUFFING

½ c. raw wild rice
Giblets from bird
1 small onion
1 tbsp. fat or salad oil
¼ lb. sausage meat
1 tsp. salt
½ tsp. powdered sage

Soak wild rice in cold water to cover overnight in the top part of the double boiler. In the morning, drain off water; place rice over boiling water and cook, covered, 10 mins. Meanwhile, clean and wash giblets, then put through a food chopper with onion, using medium blade. Melt fat in skillet and saute giblets, onion and sausage in it for 10 mins. or until sausage is cooked. Add wild rice, salt and sage, and cook for 2 mins. longer. Use to stuff body cavity of a wild pheasant weighing 1½ lbs. minus head, feet and organs.

ROAST PHEASANT

Salt
1 whole young pheasant
1 bay leaf
3 to 4 celery leaves
4 slices bacon
⅓ c. salad oil
½ c. mushroom pieces
1 large onion, sliced

Thoroughly salt pheasant inside and out; fill cavity with bay leaf and celery leaves. Wrap pheasant breast with bacon; secure in place with string. Place pheasant in roaster. Pour salad oil over pheasant. Add mushrooms and onion slices. Bake at 350 degrees for 1 hr. and 30 mins. Turn pheasant at 30 min. intervals, basting with drippings from pan. Place on platter; remove string, celery leaves and bay leaf. Garnish with spiced apples and parsley.

WILD PHEASANT ON RICE

1 pheasant, cup up
Salt and pepper
1 c. flour
1 c. shortening
1 pkg. brown gravy mix
1 pkg. onion gravy mix
1 c. rice
2 c. water

Season pheasant with salt and pepper; roll in flour, Brown in shortening in skillet; place in baking dish. Prepare brown gravy mix and onion gravy mix as directed on pkg. Pour over pheasant; cover. Bake at 300 degrees for 2 hrs. Pheasant may be cooked in pressure saucepan for 45 mins. at 15 lbs. pressure. Place rice, 1 tsp. salt and water in saucepan; cover. Bring to a boil; reduce heat and simmer for 14 mins. Serve with pheasant. Yield: 4 servings.

ROASTED PRAIRIE CHICKEN

1 dressed prairie chicken
Celery leaves
½ apple
Melted butter or margarine

Wash chicken and pat dry. Stuff cavity with celery leaves and apple. Truss into shape. Roast in 425 degree over for 30 to 40 mins. Baste frequently with melted butter or margarine. Remove stuffing before serving. Serves 2-3.

QUAIL DELIGHT

3 or 4 dressed quail
Flour
Salt and pepper
Frying oil

Gravy:

1 can mushroom soup
1 can milk
½ tsp. garlic salt
½ tsp. onion salt
1 small can chopped ripe olives
1 small can chopped pimientos

Take 3 to 4 cleaned and washed quail and cut in half. Flour each piece and salt and pepper to taste. Put in heavy skillet with oil and fry until browned. Remove from skillet; set aside. Remove oil.

Make a gravy of mushroom soup, milk, garlic salt, onion salt, olives and pimientos. Put quail back in skillet. Pour gravy over and bake 1 hr. with lid on.

ROAST QUAIL

Quail
1 grape left per quail
Salt pork, sliced
½ c. water
1 tbsp. sherry
¼ c. seedless grapes
Butter or margarine

Heat over to 450 degrees. Heat shallow pan in oven. Clean quail; wrap in grape leaves if available. Cover with slices of fat salt pork; tie in place with string. Place quail, breast side up, in heated pan; spread with butter or marg. Roast uncovered, basting often, 15-20 mins. depending on degree of rareness desired. When quail is done remove from pan; remove leaves and place under broiler a few mins. to brown. Add water to drippings in pan; simmer to loosen all bits that cling to pan. Add sherry and the seedless grapes. Serve with quail. Allow 1 bird per serving.

QUAIL WITH MUSHROOMS

6 slices bacon
6 quail, dressed
Salt and pepper
½ lb. mushroom caps
1 bunch green onions, chopped
3 tbsp. melted butter
2 tbsp. prepared mustard
½ tsp. dry ginger
1 c. orange marmalade

Wrap a slice of bacon around each quail; arrange in rows on a large sheet of heavy-duty aluminum foil. Season with salt and pepper. Saute mushroom caps and green onions in butter. Pour all over quail; seal with a double wrap. Bake at 325 degrees for 1 hr. Combine remaining ingredients; serve with quail. Yield: 6 servings.

QUAIL, SOUTHERN STYLE

2 quail
2 tbsp. flour
1 tsp. flour

2 tbsp. fat or salad oil
¾ c. light cream or top milk
1/8 tsp. pepper

Clean quail. Split down back or leave whole. Dust with combined flour, salt and pepper. Heat fat in skillet and brown quails. Add cream; cover and cook over low heat for 25 mins. or until tender. Thicken gravy, if desired. Serves 2.

SAGE GROUSE

2 sage grouse
Salt and pepper
Flour

3 tbsp. cooking oil
1 qt. half-half cream
Parsley flakes

Cut grouse into serving pieces and wash and dry with towel. Salt and pepper and dredge with flour. Place in pan containing cooking oil. Over medium heat, brown all sides. Place in baking dish, arranging close together in a single layer. Pour cream over all pieces. Sprinkle generously with parsley flakes.
Bake in preheated over, 325 degrees for 2 hrs. Check after 1 hr. to make sure

meat is not sticking to bottom of pan.

ROASTED SAGE HEN

Dressed sage hen
1 lge. onion, diced
1 clove garlic, diced
Bacon slices

Sprinkle onion and garlic over the birds, but do not stuff them. Lay bacon slices over the top of the birds. This adds moisture and holds the onions and garlic in place. Roast at 350 degrees for 2 hrs. Remove bacon, onion and serve. Unless game is cleaned when first shot it will have a very strong sage flavor.

SAGE HEN

Split thawed birds in half lengthwise or have the breasts skinned out. Soak in cold water for 30 mins. Brown floured sage hen. Add just enough water to cover birds and then add the following ingredients:

1 onion, chopped or equal amount of instant onion
½ tsp. celery salt
1 bay leaf
1 tsp. parsley
1 tbsp. lemon juice
1/8 tsp. each savory, tarragon and thyme
Pepper to taste

Bring to boil; reduce heat and simmer covered, 2 to 4 hrs. or until birds are tender.

BAKED WILD TURKEY

2 small turkeys, quartered
4 tbsp. honey
Salt and pepper
½ stick butter
½ c. chopped onion
1 c. chicken stock
1 c. white wine
1 tsp. parsley flakes

Quarter turkey; brush with honey. Shake on salt and pepper and place in shallow baking dish. Bake in hot oven (450 degrees) for 30 mins., basting often with butter. Mix onion, chicken stock, wine and parsley flakes. Pour over turkey. Reduce heat to 250 degrees. Cover. Continue baking turkey until done. Approx. 1 hr.

BAKED WILD DUCK

wild duck
thin strips of salt pork
½ c. boiling water
salt
pepper

Dress as any poultry. Wipe inside and outside with a damp cloth. If ducks are old, parboil 15 minutes. Rub inside and out with salt and pepper. Cover breast with thin strips of salt pork. Place in baking pan. Cover. Add ½ c. boiling water. Bake in hot oven (450 degrees F.) about 45 minutes, or until tender.

PARTRIDGE AND DRESSING

breast of partridge
Crisco
butter

Dressing:

½ lb. sausage
½ stick margarine
2 stalks celery
medium onion
bread
egg
sage

Dressing:
Brown sausage. Drain grease. Saute together margarine, celery, onion and sausage. Break up bread and moisten cubes with water. Add egg to bread. Season with sage. Add sausage mixture to bread mixture.

Grease bottom of casserole dish. Place dressing on bottom. Lay breasts, slit, with butter pats in slits, on top of dressing. Salt and pepper. Cover. Bake at 375 degrees for 1½ hours.

ROAST WILD DUCK

1 duck (Mallard, Black, Blue Teal or Butterball)
2 c. cubed dried bread or regular packaged stuffing
1 onion, cut up fine   ¼ tsp. dill weed
½ c. celery   salt and pepper to taste
1 c. diced apple
1 chicken bouillon dissolved in 1 c. hot water

Clean duck thoroughly and soak overnight in salt water to cover. Drain off salt water and rinse in clear water. Stuff duck and wrap up tight in heavy foil. Place in roasters pan and roast in slow oven (325 degrees) allowing 30 minutes per pound. Roasting time will vary according to age and size of duck.

*2 c. sauerkraut may be used in place of bread crumbs.

ROAST WILD GOOSE

1 wild goose
salt and pepper
1 tbsp. vinegar
1 onion
flour

Clean goose well, season with salt and pepper and vinegar. Place an onion in cavity. Let stand overnight. Remove onion. Dredge with flour and place in roasting pan in slow oven 325 degrees F. Roast uncovered until tender and browned, 20 to 25 minutes per pound, basting with juices in pan. Goose may be filled with stuffing if desired.

SMOTHERED CROW

Sportsmen learn, that the crow, as well as being an exclusive target, are good to eat. Young birds are the best.

In a skillet, fry a clove of garlic in bacon fat. Remove. Roll bird in flour and season with salt and pepper. Place in a skillet, brown on both sides, cover and occasionally add a bit of water. Cook until tender. Season with H.P. Sauce or Worcestershire Sauce. Serve.

ROAST GROUSE

Grouse are very dry birds and need larding to make them palatable. Clean bird and wipe with damp cloth. Cover completely with strips of bacon. Roast in moderate oven (350 degrees F.) until tender. About 1 hour. Baste frequently. Just before serving, remove bacon, brush bird with melted fat, dredge with flour and return to the oven to brown. Gravy is served with grouse. Use the thickened juices from the roasting pan.

QUAIL BAKED IN WINE

½ c. fat
2 small onions, minced
2 whole cloves
1 tsp. peppercorns
2 cloves garlic, cut fine
2 c. white wine
½ tsp. salt
1/8 tsp. pepper
few grains cayenne
1 tsp. minced chives

½ bay leaf   2 c. cream
6 quail, cleaned and trussed

Melt fat, add onions, cloves, peppercorns, garlic and bay leaf; cook for several minutes. Add quail and brown on all sides. Add wine, salt, pepper, cayenne and chives and simmer until tender. (about 30 minutes) Remove quail to hot serving dish. Strain sauce and add cream and heat to boiling point. Pour over quail.

CANADIAN WILD GOOSE

6-7 lb. goose   onion-celery dressing OR
½ lb. sliced mushrooms   onion-apple dressing
2 tbsp. butter   1 can consomme soup

Clean, singe, wash and dry the 6-7 lb. goose. Stuff with dressing. Bake, uncovered at 500 degrees for 30 minutes. Turn oven to 350 degrees; cover and bake 1 more hour. Meanwhile saute the mushrooms in the butter. Stir in the consomme soup. Simmer 5 minutes. Pour over goose, cover and bake about 1 hour more, or until well done. Makes about 6 servings.

*Follow package directions on ready-to-use stuffing mix.

SAUERKRAUT-STUFFED ROAST DUCK

1 quart sauerkraut   1 lb. of pork spareribs
2 apples, chopped   ¼ tsp. salt
1 medium onion, chopped   dash of pepper

Prepare duck. Soak 2 hours in solution of cold water and 1 c. vinegar. Dry and season with salt and pepper. Leave overnight in a cool, dry place. Cook together sauerkraut, apple, onion and ribs, cook until ribs fall from bones. Use this mixture as a stuffing for ducks. Cook duck until tender and golden brown.

STUFFED WILD DUCK

½ duck per person   1 egg
salt to taste   ½ c. water
celery   onion
½ package bread crumbs

Clean, singe, wash and drain duck. Sprinkle inside and outside with salt or

seasoned salt. Saute in butter, celery and onion. Add egg and ½ c. water. Mix with stuffing. Stuff duck and put into baking pan, and cover with foil. Bake at 375 degrees for 1½ hours. Uncover and turn oven to 400 degrees. Continue to bake about 1 hour, or until golden brown. Serve with cranberry orange relish and mushroom wild rice.
Note: Gravy made from drippings from mallard and other "non-fishy" ducks is excellent.

WILD DUCK A LA ORANGE

2 (1-2 lb.) ducks - split in halves lengthwise
1 medium onion - sliced & separated into rings
2 tbsp. margarine or butter
2 tbsp. frozen orange juice (concentrated, thawed)
2 tbsp. honey
1 tbsp. lemon juice
½ tsp. ginger
¼ tsp. allspice or cinnamon

Roast duck on rack in shallow roasting pan at 400 degrees for 1 hour or until tender. Season to taste placing onion rings on top.
GLAZE: Mix butter, orange juice, honey, lemon juice, ginger and allspice. Heat just to boiling. simmer 1 minute. Pour over duck, basting often. Serve hot.

ORANGE AND WALNUT STUFFED DUCK

½ c. chopped walnuts
3½ c. 1 inch bread cubes
½ c. hot water
1 egg, beaten
1½ tsp. salt
dash of pepper
¼ tsp. poultry seasoning
2 tbsp. grated orange peel
pulp of 1 large orange
1¾ c. sliced celery
¼ c. melted butter
1 (4-5 lb.) duck

Toast nuts at 300 degrees for 7 minutes; toast bread cubes at 350 degrees until brown. Pour hot water over bread; let stand for 10 minutes. Beat egg with ½ tsp., salt, pepper and poultry seasoning; combine with nuts, bread, orange peel, orange pulp and celery. Pour butter over all; toss well. Rub inside of duck with 1 tsp. salt; spoon in stuffing. Bake uncovered at 325 degrees for 2 to 2½ hours.

FRIED PRAIRIE CHICKEN

1 young prairie chicken
salt and pepper
flour
1 tbsp. butter
3 tbsp. other fat

Clean prairie chicken, dress and cut into serving pieces. Plunge into cold water, drain thoroughly but do not wipe dry. Season well with salt and pepper and dredge thickly with flour. Fry chicken slowly in hot fat until brown and tender, about 45 minutes. Make cream gravy in the skillet and serve with the chicken.

PRAIRIE CHICKEN BAKE

½ c. flour
1½ tsp. salt
¼ tsp. pepper
1 tbsp. paprika
1 (2½-3 lb.) chicken
¼ c. salad oil
½ (6 oz. can) or ⅓ c. frozen orange juice concentrate, thawed
1-8 oz. can whole onions drained
½ c. coarsely chopped carrots
1-3 oz. can sliced mushrooms drained
1 tbsp. brown sugar
¼ tsp. ground ginger

Combine first 4 ingredients in a paper or plastic bag; add 2 or 3 pieces of chicken at a time, shake. (Reserve 2 tbsp. remaining flour mixture). In a skillet, brown chicken pieces in hot oil. Remove chicken to a 2 quart casserole, add onions, carrots and mushrooms. Blend reserve flour mixture, brown sugar, ginger, dash of salt into drippings in skillet. Stir to make smooth paste. Add orange juice concentrate and ¾ c. water, cook and stir till bubbly. Pour over chicken. Cover. Bake at 350 degrees for 1¼ hours. Makes 4 servings.

PHEASANT MULLIGAN WITH DUMPLINGS

2 young pheasants
2 c. diced carrots
1 c. diced onion
1 c. finely shredded cabbage
2 c. diced potatoes
2 tbsp. fat
salt and pepper

DUMPLINGS:
2 c. sifted flour
3 tsp. baking powder
½ tsp. salt
1 egg
¾ c. milk

Clean pheasants, cut into serving portions and cover with water. Add carrots, onions, cabbage and cook slowly until nearly tender. Add potatoes, fat, salt and pepper. Cook until meat and vegetables are tender. Make dumplings as follows: sift flour, baking powder and salt together; beat eggs, add milk and stir into dry ingredients adding more milk if necessary to form a drop batter. Drop by tablespoon into hot mulligan and cover kettle tightly. Cook for 15 minutes without lifting the cover.

PHEASANT SUPREME

¾ c. butter
½ c. flour
4 c. milk
½ tsp. salt
¼ tsp. pepper
1 can green asparagus

1 c. grated aged cheese
1 can pimento, chopped
4 c. cooked pheasant, chopped
3 c. ritz cracker crumbs
4 hard cooked eggs, chopped

Melt ½ c. butter, blend in flour. Add milk and seasonings, stirring constantly; cook until thickened. Add eggs, cheese and pimento. Place 1 c. ritz crumbs in a lightly buttered 2 quart casserole; add a layer of white sauce, pheasant and asparagus. Repeat layer ending with white sauce; top with crumbs. Pour ¼ c. melted butter over top. Bake at 350 degrees for 30 minutes or until top is browned.

SOUTH DAKOTA ROAST PHEASANT

1 pheasant, cut into serving pieces
1 tsp. salt
½ c. cooking oil

white cooking wine (optional)
¾ c. flour
¼ tsp. pepper
1 c. sweet or sour cream

Dredge pheasant in flour seasoned with salt and pepper; brown in hot oil. Arrange in covered casserole; add cream. Bake, covered, at 375 degrees for 2 hours or until tender. Add water as needed; baste occasionally with cream and drippings. Add a small amount of white wine the last 30 minutes of baking time to tenderize and add flavor.

BAKED PHEASANT WITH RICE

Breasts, legs and thighs of 2 pheasants
¾ c. uncooked rice
1 tbsp. grated onion
2 tsp. chicken stock base
½ stick butter (¼ lb.)

salt and pepper to taste
1-3 oz. can mushrooms
2 c. water

Roll pheasant in flour and brown. Cut breasts in half. Place rice, salt and pepper into large greased casserole and add onion. Add mushrooms and juice. Place pheasant on rice mixture, add chicken stock, dissolved in water. Dot with butter. Bake at 300 degrees for 1½ hours. Serves 4 - 6.
*Wild rice may be used.

PHEASANT A LA LORRAINE

1 c. finely chopped
   scallions - with top
1 c. chicken bouillon
1 tsp. salt
1½ c. heavy cream

½ c. butter
1 pheasant, cut in half
1 sliced carrot
pepper to taste
3 tbsp. horseradish

Cook scallions in ¼ c. butter in heavy iron skillet over low heat until soft, but not brown. Remove from heat. Add rest of butter and pheasant. Cover and cook over low heat until golden brown on both sides. Put pheasant into baking dish. Add scallions, bouillon, carrot, salt and pepper. Cover and bake 1 hour, basting frequently. Remove pheasant. Pour a mixture of cream and horseradish into the baking dish. Stir gently. Put pheasant in sauce in pan. Bake, uncovered for 30 minutes in 275 degree oven. Place pheasant on serving platter. Strain sauce, salt to taste and serve in sauce boat. If desired the sauce may be flamed by heating ½ c. French brandy, light by match and pour over pheasant. Serves 4-5.

BARBECUED PHEASANT

1 pheasant, cut up
½ c. oil
2 tsp. salt
1 tsp. pepper
1 tbsp. paprika
½ c. flour

¾ c. water
¾ c. ketchup
2 tbsp. grated onion
1 tsp. garlic salt
1 tsp. chopped parsley

Combine oil, salt, pepper and paprika. Dip pheasant in oil mixture, roll in flour. Place in flat pan. Mix water, ketchup, onion, garlic and parsley; bring to boil. Pour over pheasant. Bake at 300-325 degrees for 1 hours.

DEVILED BIRDS

Here is a good way to get rid of your left-overs:
Mix:
   ½ oz. butter
   ½ tsp. mustard
   ¼ tsp. cayenne

   ½ tsp. salt
   dash of pepper or
   ¼ tsp. chili powder

Cut the meat fine. Add mixture and heat well in fry pan.

SESAME RICE STUFFINGS FOR PRAIRIE CHICKEN

½ c. chopped celery
2 tbsp. margarine
3 tbsp. sesame seeds
1 tbsp. dried onion flakes

1 tbsp. dried parsley flakes
½ tsp. salt
dash dried thyme
2 c. cooked rice

Cook ½ c. chopped celery in 2 tbsp. margarine or butter till tender, but not brown. Mix in 3 tbsp. sesame seeds, toasted, 1 tbsp. dried onion flakes, 1 tbsp. dried parsley flakes, ½ tsp. salt with dash of thyme. Combine with 2 c. cooked long-grained rice, tossing lightly till mixed. Makes 2 c. rice stuffing; enough for 5 lbs. chicken, partridge or duck.

SAUCE FOR WILD DUCK

1 c. red currant jelly
1 tbsp. Worcestershire sauce

salt & pepper to taste
¼ c. orange juice
1 tbsp. dry mustard

Simmer all ingredients and pour over duck.

WILD GOOSE

1 wild goose
salt and pepper
2 apples, sliced
1 onion, sliced

2 stalks celery, chopped
bacon drippings
4 bacon slices

Rub inside of goose with salt and pepper. Stuff loosely with sliced onion, apple and celery. Brush bacon drippings or margarine lightly over entire body. Place bacon slices over breast. Roast in 325 degree oven in covered roaster, adding 2 c. liquid ro roaster or wrap breast in aluminum foil and roast in open pan, adding liquid. Baste frequently. Roast 15 mins. per lb. or until tender. Remove stuffing and serve.

SAUCY APPLE GOOSE

1 wild goose, dressed
2 applies, peeled and sliced
1 can applesauce
¼ c. currant jelly
1 tsp. cinnamon
1 tsp. nutmeg
½ c. corn syrup

Place 2 cooking apples, peeled and sliced in cavity of goose. Bake in 350 degree oven for 20 to 25 mins. per lb. While baking, baste frequently with a sauce made by heating together applesauce, jelly, cinnamon, syrup and nutmeg. Serve the sauce as a gravy separately or over carved bird. Serves 4.

ROASTED WILD GOOSE WITH SAUERKRAUT

1 wild goose, dressed
sauerkraut
butter
salt and pepper

Stuff the goose with sauerkraut and rub a little butter on the outside. Salt and pepper. Bake at 350 degrees until tender. Serve the sauerkraut with the goose. The goose will not taste of the kraut; it only makes it moist and improves the flavor.

ROAST GOOSE

1 wild goose, dressed
½ c. pancake flour
½ c. regular flour
salt, pepper, paprika
fat sufficient for browning
onion, sliced
bacon slices

Cut wild goose in serving pieces, splitting breast, Shake or roll the pieces in the seasoned flour mixture. Brown in hot fat in iron Dutch oven. Arrange the pieces in layers with sliced onion. Put slices of bacon over top and bake covered at 350 degrees for 2½ to 3 hrs. Makes a delicious gravy.

ROAST WILD DUCK

1 wild duck or 2 ducks - to make 4 to 6 lbs.
1 tbsp. soy sauce
1 tbsp. sugar
2 tbsp. honey
3 tbsp. dry sherry
1 tsp. salt
½ tsp. monosodium glutamate

Combine soy sauce, sugar, honey and sherry. Rub outside of duck with this mixture and let stand for an hour, turning occasionally or leave in the refrigerator overnight. Rub inside of duck with salt and monosodium glutamate. Place duck in open pan and roast at 300 degrees for ½ hour. Then cook duck with foil to delay browning. Continue roasting duck for another hour. Remove foil and raise temperature of oven to 400 degrees for 15 mins.

ROAST WILD DUCK

    2 wild mallard ducks
    1 tsp. salt
    ½ tsp. pepper
    ¼ tsp. rosemary leaves
    1 med. onion, cut into eighths
    1 apple, cut into eighths
    2 stalks celery, cut up
    ½ c. butter or margarine, melted
    ¼ tsp. pepper
    ¼ tsp. rosemary leaves

Heat oven to 350 degrees.
Clean ducks; wash and pat dry. Stir together salt, ½ tsp. pepper and ¼ tsp. rosemary leaves; sprinkle in cavity and on outside of each duck. Place half the onion, half the apple and half the celery in each cavity. Place ducks breast side down on rack in open shallow roasting pan. Roast 40 mins. Combine butter, ¼ tsp. pepper and ¼ tsp. rosemary leaves; baste ducks frequently during roasting. Turn ducks and roast 50 min. longer or until done. Ducks are done when juices are no longer pink when cut between leg and body. Remove ducks from pan; split in half lengthwise. Discard stuffing. Yield: 4 servings.

MALLARD SUPREME

    Dressed duck
    Seasoned flour (salt and pepper)
    ¼ lb. margarine
    1 lge. can condensed milk

Cut the duck in small pieces for frying as you do chicken. Roll in seasoned flour. Place the margarine in roaster or heavy pan. Brown the floured pieces on both sides. Pour condensed milk over this and cover. Cook in 375 degree oven until tender. If it begins to get dry, add a small amount of water. Discard the condensed milk mixture and serve only the meat. Very different, rich and tasty.

OVEN-BAKED DUCK

    2 ducks (mallard size)
    1 can onion soup
    shortening

Cut duck into parts as you would do for a chicken. Brown these pieces in a cast-iron skillet with ½ to ¾" of melted shortening. When all pieces are well browned, lay the breasts meat side down, in the skillet and put the other parts around the breasts. Pour onion soup over the browned meat and cover the skillet. Place in 250 degree oven and bake for 2 hours. Serves four.

BROILED WILD DUCK

One 1½-lb. wild mallard duck, halved
baking soda (opt.)
¼ c. butter or margarine, melted
1 tsp. salt
¼ c. melted currant jelly

Rinse duck thoroughly; pat dry with paper towels. If desired, rub entire surface of duck with 1 tbsp. baking soda; rinse thoroughly. Place duck, skin side down, on broiler rack. Combine butter and salt with 2 tbsp. water; brush duck with part of mixture. Broil 6" from heat for 5 to 15 mins., depending on desired doneness. Brush occasionally with butter mixture. Turn duck; broil for 5 to 15 mins. longer, brushing occasionally with butter mixture. Remove; brush with currant jelly. Yield: 2 servings.

BARBECUED MALLARDS

4 mallard ducks, dressed
1 c. orange marmalade
½ c. orange juice
1 tbsp. soy sauce
1 tsp. basil
1 tsp. salt
¼ tsp. fresh ground pepper
Cornstarch

Broil ducks on rotisserie for 50 mins. to 1 hr. Combine remaining ingredients except cornstarch in a saucepan; bring to a boil. Make a thin paste of cornstarch and water. Gradully add to orange mixture, stirring continuously. Cook until mixture coats a spoon. Baste duck with sauce 3 times during the last 30 mins. of cooking time. Yield: 4 servings.

DUCK AND POTATOES

1 wild duck, cleaned
1 unpeeled apple, cut into halves
salt and pepper to taste
4 to 5 lge. potatoes, diced
1 lge. onion
2 to 3 tbsp. dry leaf sage

Place whole duck and apple in a 5-qt. kettle with 3 to 4 c. water; cover. Boil for 30 mins. Discard water and apple. Add 3 to 4 c. water to parboiled duck; salt and pepper to season. Cover. Bake at 350 degrees for 45 mins. Add potatoes, onion, sage and seasonings. Bake for 45 mins. to 1 hr. or until duck and potatoes are tender. If necessary, add water as there should be sufficient liquid on duck and potatoes. Yield: 6 servings.

SMOTHERED DOVES

Salt and pepper
3 dove breasts
½ c. flour
8 tbsp. fat

4 tsp. Worcestershire sauce
4 tsp. lemon juice
1 c. water

Salt and pepper doves. Put flour in paper bag. Drop breasts into flour. Close bag; shake well. Melt fat in skillet. Fry doves in fat until golden brown. Put ½ tsp. lemon juice on top of each dove. Add 1 c. water; cover skillet. Simmer for 1 hr. or until tender. Add water if necessary. Service with rice. Yield: 4 servings.

HUNTER'S BOOYA

4 wild ducks - cleaned
   and halved
6 lb. venison
2 lb. cubed pork
2½ lb. soup bones
4 large sliced onions
2 c. parsley sprigs
½ c. dry split peas
½ c. dry lima beans
¼ c. salt

2 tbsp. pepper
2 tbsp. garlic salt
1 tbsp. dried crushed basil
1 tbsp. dried crushed oregano
1 tsp. dried crushed savory

In a very large kettle, combine meat, ducks, soup bones, onions, parsley, split peas, lima beans and seasons. Add water to cover. Bring to a boil. Reduce heat, cover, and simmer 4-5 hrs. or until meat is tender.

Remove meat from bones and cube. Discard bones, skim fat from stock and return meat to kettle.

Add:
    3 c. diced carrots
    3 c. diced celery

1 large head red cabbage, coarsely chopped
3 c. diced rutabaga
1 c. diced green pepper

Simmer cover for 1 hr. Add -

3-28 oz. cans tomatoes, undrained
3-15½ oz. cans cut green beans, undrained
2-10 oz. pkg. frozen peas
2-10 oz. pkg. frozen whole kernel corn

Simmer covered 1 hr. more. Serves 30-35 generously.

WILD ACRES PHEASANT OR MALLARD AND WILD RICE

1 c. wild rice
4 c. water
3-4 tsp. sage
¼ lb. margarine
4-5 stalks diced celery
1 med. onion
1 can cream of mushroom soup
¾ tbsp. soy sauce

Salt and pepper bird. Roast in 400 degree oven for 1 hr. or until done. Baste with margarine and soy sauce.

Prepare wild rice. Mix 1 c. rice, water and sage. Bring to a boil. Cover and simmer about 30 min. Fluff with a fork. Turn off heat (1 c. rice makes 3 c.). Saute ¼ lb. margarine, celery and onion. Take meat off bones. Save the breasts whole. Add meat pieces and stock from roaster pan, cream of mushroom soup and ¾ tbsp. soy sauce to saute mix. Simmer 10 min.

Layer in casserole rice and sauteed mixture. Place breasts on top. Dot with margarine and sprinkle with soy sauce.

Cover and bake 20 min. Makes 5-6 large servings.

DELTA DUCK A LA STE. THERESE

8 duck breast halves (4 ducks)
½ lb. fresh mushrooms (sliced)
5 sweet pickled onions
1 med. onion (finely chopped)
2 cloves garlic (finely chopped)
1 bay leaf
½ c. Madeira wine
3 tbsp. margarine

Soak duck breasts overnight in buttermilk. Preheat oven to 325 degrees. Rinse breasts with water and pat dry. Melt margarine in fry pan. Sear breasts on each side quickly. Place in 3 qt. casserole with bay leaf. In same fry pan saute garlic, onion and pickled onions. Add Madeira wine and pour over ducks. Add salt and pepper and cover. Bake 1½ hours. Just before serving saute mushrooms and a few sprigs of chopped parsley for a few minutes and garnish ducks with same.

PLUM SAUCE WILD GOOSE

1 (5-6 lb.) goose
salt and pepper
2 tbsp. sugar
1¼ tsp. salt
½ c. plum sauce
3 tbsp. dark soy sauce
4 cloves garlic, crushed
3 green onions cut in 2 in. pieces
2 large pieces dried orange peel or
    ½ tsp. grated fresh orange peel
¼ cup sherry
1-1½ c. water
pepper to taste

Clean and remove all the fat around the cavity of the goose. Rub inside with salt and pepper. Mix all remaining ingredients together. Pour over goose and let marinate at least 3 hours. Roast the goose in the sauce at 350 degrees F. for 20 to 25 mins. per pound. Turn goose and baste it with sauce several times during roasting. If the sauce thickens too much, add a little water and continue roasting until tender. Lift goose out of the roast pan and cut in pieces. Keep warm on a hot platter. Skim fat from the sauce in the roast pan. There should be about 1 cup sauce left in the pan. If not, add a little boiling water or extra sherry and stir well. Then pour over the goose. Makes enough for 4 servings.

Fish

FISH

BAKED WINNIPEG GOLDEYE (SMOKED)

Allow one goldeye per serving.

Wipe the required numbered of goldeyes with a damp cloth. Sprinkle inside of each fish with black pepper and melted butter. Arrange in a shallow buttered baking dish and spread melted butter over the top. Bake at 400 degrees F. for about 10 to 15 minutes, basting occasionally. Remove skin and serve on a hot platter with parsley and lemon wedges.

Note: Remove heads before or after baking.

STUFFED LAKE TROUT

1 large lake trout
butter
salt and pepper
cherry

Stuffing:
½ c. butter
1 small onion, chopped
3 tbsp. celery, chopped
4 c. bread, cubed
1 tsp. sage or poultry seasoning
1 tsp. salt
½ tsp. pepper
4 tbsp. parsley

Stuffing:
Melt butter and slowly cook onions and celery until golden brown. Add bread crumbs and remaining ingredients. Toss lightly so all ingredients are mixed well. Place tinfoil on cookie sheet. Place fish on it. Open fish wide and stuff all of stuffing into it. Salt and butter and pepper skin of trout. Place a tinfoil tent over fish. Bake at 375 degrees for 2 hours. (Depending on size of fish).

The eye of the fish will come out while baking. When fish is ready to serve place a cherry in the eye hole and serve on lettuce leaves for a fancy appearance.

*Be sure to baste fish while it is cooking. Placing butter on the bottom side before adding stuffing will prevent necessity of basting while cooking.

FRIED SMELT

1 dozen smelt   Crisco (¾ pan full)

Batter:

salt and pepper   1 c. Bisquick
water to make thin   ¼ tsp. sage
1 egg

Heat Crisco until it sizzles. Dip cleaned smelt in batter and place in oil. When batter is golden brown, remove and place on paper towels.

BAKED WHITE FISH OR TROUT

your favorite sage dressing   onion
fish   salt
1 c. milk   pepper

Make sage dressing and stuff fish. Put 1 c. canned or whole milk in bottom of roaster. Lay fish in. Top with sliced onions and salt and pepper. Bake at 350 degrees for 45-50 minutes.

PIKE OR COHO

1 fish, filleted/per package
butter   pepper
seasoned salt   tin foil

In tin foil, place fish steaks. Butter, salt and pepper both sides of steaks. Seal tin foil on ends and middle. Bake at 375 degrees for 1 hour.

BAKED FISH SUPREME

2-3 lbs. fillets of fish (preferably whitefish,
    but can use menominee, trout, pike)

olive oil (MUST be this)   6 ribs celery
4 cloves garlic   2 green peppers
2 medium onions   4 medium ripe tomatoes
4-6 carrots (fresh)   (fresh)
4-5 medium sized potatoes   1 lemon
    (fresh)   salt, pepper & oregano

*I prefer an electric roaster, but any heavy roaster may be used, with tight fitting top.

Cover bottom of roaster with olive oil. Lay fish fillets side by side in bottom of roaster, skin side down. Sprinke with salt and pepper and 2 cloves of garlic, cut up fine. Cover with a layer of onions, next a layer of celery, sliced fine; then a layer of potatoes, sliced thin; next a layer of carrots, sliced thin; next a layer of sliced ripe tomatoes; next a layer of green pepper rings. Now slice the lemon thin and place on top. Cut up 2 cloves garlic and scatter over top. Sprinkle with salt and pepper and oregano over entire roaster. Bake at 300 degrees until vegetables feel soft when tried with a fork. Use large serving spatula to dish out. (Makes a complete meal).

TROUT WITH GRAPEFRUIT

trout
butter
slivered almonds

2 tbsp. grapefruit juice
2 tbsp. chopped parsley

Bake trout, brushed with melted butter in 450 degree oven about 10 minutes, until fish flakes easily with a fork. Heat together ¼ c. butter, ¼ c. slivered almonds, grapefruit juice and parsley, to make a sauce. Surround with grapefruit sections and pour sauce all over.

*Taken from Better Homes and Gardens.

TROUT PIE

Bake in 400 degree oven.

Rich pie crust:
    2 c. flour
    4 tbsp. Crisco
    ½ tsp. salt
    ½ c. ice water

Cream Sauce:
    6 heaping tbsp. flour
    3 heaping tbsp. butter
    2 tbsp. chopped chives, fine
    ½ tsp. paprika
    salt and pepper to taste
    1½ qt. milk
    ½ pt. heavy cream

6 lb. trout (salmon may be substitued for trout)
10 hardboiled eggs, sliced

Put trout in large pot and cover with boiling water. Add 1 tbsp. salt and steam for about 5 mins. Skin and bone trout. In large 4 qt. baking dish put a layer of trout and cover with 2 layers of the sliced hardboiled eggs, then another layer of trout and 2 layers of sliced eggs. Repeat trout and eggs, until dish is about ¾ filled. Pour in cream sauce to cover trout and eggs; on top, cover with rich pie crust. Bake in 400 degree oven until crust is golden.

BAKED FISH IN TOMATO DILL SAUCE

1 lb. fish fillets (such as perch)
1 c. chopped onion
2 tbsp. butter
1 tbsp. flour
1 can condensed consomme, undiluted
½ c. tomato catsup
¾ c. sliced dill pickle

Heat oven to 400 degrees. Saute onions in butter. Stir in flour; gradually add consomme and catsup. Simmer for 25 mins., stirring occasionally. Add pickles. Place fish in baking dish (10x6x1½"); cover with sauce. Bake 25-30 mins. or until fish flakes easily with a fork. Yield: 4 servings.

CRAWDAD BOIL
(CRAWFISH)

2 dozen or more crawfish
Salt
Butter

Bring a kettle of salted water (½ c. salt to 1 gallon water) to a rolling boil; pop in the crawfish and simmer until then turn a deep red. Break off the tails; serve like shrimp and let each one shuck out his own meat. Serve with melted butter flavored with lemon juice and just a hint of mint.

(Check the game laws because some states require a fishing license to gather crawfish).

PAN FRIED WHITE BASS

6 small white bass
1 c. buttermilk
Juice of 1 lemon
½ c. cornmeal
½ c. instant mashed potatoes
¼ tsp. pepper
½ tsp. salt
2 c. shortening

Soak fish overnight in buttermilk and lemon juice. Roll fish in a mixture of cornmeal and mashed potato flakes, plus salt and pepper. Heat shortening until piping hot. Add fish and cook until brown, approx. 8 to 10 mins. on each side. These fish are delicious fried.

POACHED WALLEYE

3 lbs. walleye, fresh
2 tsp. salt
1 tsp. pepper
4 tbsp. water
3 tbsp. butter
4 tbsp. lemon juice
1 small onion, minced
1 sprig parsley, minced

Fillet fish; rub in salt and pepper. Drizzle lemon juice over fillets. Then spread with butter. Sprinkle on onion and parsley. Add water; wrap in foil and place over med. barbecue coals for 20 mins. Turn occasionally.

PICKLED BULLHEADS

Bullheads
4 med. onions
5 to 6 bay leaves
1 tbsp. whole pickling spice
2 c. vinegar
1½ c. water
1 tbsp. salt
Pepper

Cut up onions; put on bottom of small roaster; add bay leaves and whole pickling spice. Lay skinned bullheads over this close together. May use more than 1 layer. Cover with a solution of 2 c. vinegar and 1½ c. water and 1 tbsp. salt and pepper. Cover and boil slowly until fish are cooked. Cool in roaster until cold. Serve cold.

BOILED FISH

Heat to rolling boil in 8 qt. kettle the following:

    4 qts. water   4 to 6 bay leaves
    2 tbsp. salt   3 to 4 shakes tabasco sauce

Add:
    2 to 3 lbs. fish, cut in 2 x 4" fillets.

Cook until tender or starting to flake. DO NOT OVERCOOK. Serve on a hot tray with lemon slices and parsley. Spread some hot lemon butter over fish on the tray and sprinkle with paprika.

Lemon Butter:
Melt ¼ lb. butter with juice of ½ lemon. (Use the other ½ lemon for the slices on the tray with fish.)

SOUTHERN BROILED TROUT

    Salt and pepper
    4 lge. fresh speckled trout
    ½ c. melted butter
    ⅓ c. lemon juice
    5 tbsp. chopped parsley
    ½ c. grated onion
    ½ tsp. paprika
    5 tbsp. Worcestershire sauce
    Few grains cayenne pepper

Salt and pepper fish; place on foil. Combine remaining ingredients; pour over fish. Close foil. Broil in oven at 450 degrees until done. Yield: 6 servings.

BAKED TROUT

    2-12 oz. pkg. frozen trout, thawed
    ¼ c. butter or margarine
    ¼ c. finely chopped celery
    1 tsp. salt
    ¼ tsp. pepper
    1 tbsp. lemon juice
    ¼ c. chopped sweet mixed pickles

Arrange trout in greased 1½ qt. shallow baking dish. Melt butter over low heat. Add celery and cook until tender. Add remaining ingredients; mix. Pour over trout. Bake at 350 degrees for 20 to 25 mins. or until fish is tender. Garnish with lemon slices and parsley, if desired. Yield: 4 servings.

BEER BATTER

Equal amounts of flour and beer. Get fish fillets and dip in batter. Put in deep fryer until golden brown and crispy. Add salt and eat away!

ex. ½ c. flour & ½ c. beer

HERBED STUFFED TROUT

½ c. chopped onion
¼ c. plus 3 tbsp. butter
1 c. dry bread crumbs
1 tsp. summer savory
1 tsp. chervil
4 trout
Monosodium glutamate
1 tbsp. lemon juice

Saute onion in 3 tbsp. butter until clear, but not brown. Remove from heat; add bread crumbs, savory and chervil. Sprinkle trout inside and out with monosodium glutamate. Fill with bread crumb mixture. Melt remaining butter; stir in lemon juice.
Bake trout at 350 degrees for 35 mins. or until fish flakes easily with a fork, basting every 5 mins. with lemon butter. Yield: 4 servings.

LAKE TROUT OR DAM TROUT

2 to 3 lbs. dressed trout
6 slices bacon
1 thinly sliced onion
1 bay leaf, crushed
3 tbsp. soft butter
2 tbsp. flour
½ c. fine cracker crumbs

Heat oven to 375 degrees. Sprinkle trout well with salt and pepper. Spread 3 bacon slices along center of pan. Cover with onion; sprinkle with bay leaf; place trout on top. Blend butter with flour and spread on fish. Place trout on top. Sprinkle with crumbs. Place 3 more bacon slices on fish. Bake uncovered 35 to 45 mins. or until golden brown and flaky.

TROUT GERMAN STYLE

Trout   Salt
Chopped onion or onion slat Celery salt

Place several (10-12") trout on wire rack in electric skillet. Pour water over them to partially cover. Sprinkle with onion, salt and celery salt. Cover and cook approx. 10 mins. Serve immediately with melted butter.

DEEP FRIED LAKE TROUT

12 lake trout   Cracker crumbs, finely
Seasoned flour   crushed
2 eggs   Deep fat for frying
4 tbsp. water

Clean and chill medium-sized lake trout. Use chore girl to remove scales. Leave whole unless they are over 9" in length. Otherwise, split lengthwise. Drain well. Beat eggs with water. First: roll trout in seasoned flour. Second: dip trout in egg mixture. Third: roll in cracker crumbs. Fry until brown in oil, 375 degrees for about 5-7 mins. Serve with potato salad and a hot buttered vegetable.

NORTHERN PIKE

4 fillets of northern pike (12-18" long)
2 c. pancake mix
1 King-size bottle 7-up
Deep fat for frying

Cut fillets into 1" square pieces. Take a pair of pliers and remove all bones from these pieces. "This is a tedious chore, but the results are well worth it." After making sure all bones are removed, add enough 7-up to the pancake mix to make a sticky batter. Dip the cut-up and boned pieces of fish into the batter and then into a deep fat fryer when fat is at 350 degrees. Fry until pancake batter is golden brown all over. Serve with a cocktail sauce, soda crackers, butter and a favorite cold beverage.

GOLDEN BROILED FISH STEAKS

2 lb. fish steaks
1 tbsp. grated onion
2 tbsp. lemon juice
¼ c. butter, melted

1 tsp. salt
dash of pepper
¼ tsp. thyme
paprika or parsley

Place steaks on greased broiler pan. Combine next 6 ingredients to make a butter sauce. Baste steaks with half the sauce. Broil for 4 to 5 minutes, turn, baste with remaining sauce and continue broiling until done. Garnish with paprika or parsley.

BAKED FISH WITH PINEAPPLE

½ c. cubed or crushed pineapple
2 c. cooked flaked fish
3/8 c. cream
¼ tsp. salt
1/8 tsp. pepper

1 c. mashed potatoes
1 egg, beaten
2 tbsp. milk
few grains of paprika
¼ c. grated cheese

Line greased casserole with drained pineapple. Combine flaked fish with cream, salt and pepper and place on top of pineapple. Beat together potatoes, egg, milk and cream, and paprika and spread over the fish mixture. Bake in moderate oven 350 degrees for 15 to 20 minutes. Top with grated cheese just before removing from oven.

BARBECUED FILLETS

2 lb. fresh fish fillets
½ c. melted butter
2 tbsp. lemon juice
¼ c. tomato catsup
¼ tsp. dry mustard

1 tsp. Worcestershire sauce
1 tsp. salt
2 tbsp. minced onion
parsley

Place fillets on a greased broiler pan. Combine butter, lemon juice, catsup, Worcestershire sauce, mustard, salt and onion. Heat mixture and pour over fillets. Place under preheated broiler 2 to 4 inches from the source of heat. Broil fish on one side only. Garnish with parsley.

OVEN STEAMED FISH

2 lbs. fish fillets
¼ tsp. salt
dash of pepper
1 tsp. lemon juice

Sprinkle fish with salt and pepper. Wrap fish tightly in envelope of greased foil. Make double folds in foil and pinch foil to make steam tight. Place on shallow pan or baking sheet and bake in a very hot oven 450-500 degrees.

GOLDEN FISH BAKE

2 lbs. fish fillets
4 tbsp. flour
1 tsp. salt
¼ tsp. pepper
1 c. milk
1 c. soft bread crumbs
4 tbsp. butter or margarine
1 tsp. dill seed
1 c. sour cream
1 lemon, sliced
parsley

Cut fillets into serving portions. Coat with flour and sprinkle with salt and pepper. Arrange in greased baking pan, pour milk over fish. Bake in moderate oven 350 degrees F. for 30 minutes. Toast crumbs in fat in frying pan. Stir dill seed into sour cream. Remove fish from oven, spread with cream mixture, top with toasted crumbs. Bake 5 minutes longer or until sour cream is set. Garnish with lemon slices and parsley.

PANFRIED WHITEFISH

2 lbs. whitefish fillets
1 tsp. salt
½ c. milk
½ c. flour
1 c. fine dried bread crumbs

Cut fish into serving size pieces. Dip in salted milk and then in flour. Dip in milk again and then in bread crumbs. Use about ¼ inch hot fat in frying pan. Fry quickly on one side, then turn and brown on the other side. Allow about 10 minutes for each 1 inch of thickness of fish.

WINE POACHED TROUT

2 or 3 rainbow trout
¼ tsp. dill seeds
¼ tsp. rosemary
1/8 tsp. seasoning salt
½ c. dry white wine
salad greens

Clean trout and remove heads, tails and fins. Add seasonings to wine and poach trout for 15 to 20 minutes or until done. Allow fish to cook in poaching liquid. Remove skin and lift fillets from bones. Serve trout on crisp salad greens with Mayonnaise Dressing.

RAINBOW TROUT WITH LEMON

6 pan ready trout
¼ c. French Dressing
salt
12 thin lemon slices

Preheat oven to 450 degrees F. Thaw fish, if frozen. Wash and pat dry with paper towel. Brush inside with French Dressing; Sprinkle with salt. Cut 6 lemon slices in half and place 2 halves in each cavity. Place fish in greased baking dish. Place a lemon on each fish and brush tops of fish with remaining French Dressing. Bake at 450 degrees F. for 10 minutes or until fish flakes easily.

GLORI-FRIED RAINBOW TROUT

4 dressed trout
salt
¼ c. flour
oil for frying
½ c. butter
1 tsp. lemon juice
¼ tsp. salt
1 small clove garlic, minced
¼ c. finely chopped parsley
¼ c. finely chopped almonds

Thaw fish if frozen. Prepare nut butter; cream butter; blend in lemon juice salt, garlic, parsley, chopped almonds. Let stand at room temperature for 1 hour before serving. Wash fish, pat dry. Sprinkle inside with salt then roll fish in flour. Fry in ¼ inch hot oil over moderate heat for 4 to 5 minutes until golden brown. Turn and fry until fish flakes easily to a fork. Drain, transfer to a heated platter and top each fish with some nut butter.

BAKED PIKE FILLETS

1 lb. pike fillets
¼ tsp. salt
few grains of pepper
½ c. butter
½ c. bread crumbs or
½ c. grated cheese
1 tsp. lemon juice

Cut fillets in portion sizes. Season with salt and pepper. Lightly brown butter in the oven in baking dish. Dip fish in browned butter and roll in crumbs or grated cheese. Sprinkle with lemon. Bake in a hot oven 450 degrees. Allow 10 minutes cooking time for each thickness of 1 inch of fish. If fish is frozen, double the cooking time. Baste occasionally with browned butter during baking.

FRIED PICKEREL

2 lbs. pickerel fillets
½ tsp. garlic salt
¼ c. fat for frying
1 tbsp. chopped celery
1 tsp. salt

½ c. instant mashed
    potato powder
½ c. chicken broth
1 tbsp. chopped green onion

Cut fillets into serving size portions. Add salt and garlic salt, to instant mashed potato powder. Dip fish in potato powder (mixture). Brown fish on both sides in fat. Reduce heat and add remaining ingredients. Simmer in a covered frying pan for 5 to 10 minutes until fish is almost cooked. Remove cover for last few minutes of cooking for a crisp coating.

PANFRIED SALMON

2 lbs. salmon
½ tsp. salt
¼ tsp. pepper
½ c. flour

4 tsp. lemon juice
2 tbsp. chopped parsley
6 tbsp. butter
salad oil for frying

Cut fish into serving size pieces. Season with salt and pepper. Dust lightly with flour. Fry in ¼ inch of hot salad oil, until brown, about 5 minutes on each side. Place fish on heated platter. Sprinkle fish with lemon juice and parsley. Drain oil from pan. In cleaned frying pan, heat butter until it browns nicely and begins to smell of nuts. Put over fish and serve immediately while butter is still foaming.

PANFRIED PERCH FILLETS

2 lbs. perch fillets
½ tsp. salt
½ tsp. poultry seasoning

½ c. milk
1/8 tsp. pepper
½ c. flour

Dip fish in milk and then in seasoned flour. Fry in about ¼ inch hot fat until brown on one side, turn and brown on the other side. Allow about 3 or 4 minutes on each side.

EGG AND LEMON SAUCE

3 whole eggs
1 c. lukewarm water or fish stock
1 tbsp. cornstarch
juice of 1 lemon

Beat the eggs until they are well blended and frothy. Add liquid, and cornstarch mixed with lemon juice. Beat well, then stir constantly over low heat until mixture is slightly thickened and smooth (don't boil).

FISH HASH

Cold cooked fish fillets (at least 1 cup)
Equal quanity of cold boiled potatoes
1 large onion, grated
¼ tsp. sage
1 egg, beaten
3 tbsp. margarine

Flake the fish and cut the potatoes into small pieces. Mix with onion, add sage and beaten egg. Melt margarine in a large frying pan. When hot, press the hash in and cook over medium heat until crusty brown underneath. Invert on to a hot platter and sprinkle to taste with minced parsley or green onions, or catsup. If the hash has been frozen, thaw it over low heat then raise heat to medium and continue.

FISHBURGERS

1 lb. ground fish - any
1 tbsp. lemon juice
¼ c. flour
½ tsp. salt
1/8 tsp. pepper
6 split, heated hamburger buns
lettuce
mayonnaise
6 tomato slices

Sprinkle ground fish with lemon juice. Combine flour, salt and pepper. Coat or mix into ground fish. Panfry in about ¼ inch hot oil or melted butter until patties are lightly browned. In each bun arrange crisp lettuce, fish pattie, mayonnaise and a slice of tomato. Serve hot.

BISCUIT-TOPPED FILLET STEW

1 pkg. frozen or fresh fish fillets
1 c. sliced carrots
1½ c. cubed potatoes
1 can refrigerated biscuits
2 tbsp. finely chopped green pepper
1½ tsp. salt

1 c. sliced onions
1 c. sliced celery
2 tbsp. finely chopped
    pimento
1½ c. water
3 tbsp. butter, melted
3 tbsp. flour
¼ tsp. poultry seasoning

Cut fillets into chunks. Place vegetables in a sauce pan, add salt and water. Cover and simmer for 10 minutes. Add chunks of fish. Cover and simmer until fish is cooked. Drain and measure broth. Add water if necessary to make 1½ cups. Place drained fish and vegetables in a greased 2 quart baking dish. Combine melted butter, flour and poultry seasoning. Add broth gradually. Cook and stir over low heat until thickened. Pour over fish and vegetables. Open can of biscuits as directed. Arrange biscuits around edge of baking dish. Bake in 425 degree oven for 15-20 minutes or until biscuits are golden brown.

BROILED TROUT KABOBS

2 lbs. trout steaks
1 c. chili sauce
⅓ c. salad oil
¼ c. lemon juice
2 tbsp. brown sugar
2 tsp. celery salt
1/8 tsp. Tabasco sauce

Remove skins and bones from trout and cut into 1 inch cubes. Combine remaining ingredients to make a sauce. Marinate trout cubes in sauce for several hours, then drain and serve on skewers. Broil over coals or in broiler, turning and basting occasionally with sauce, until trout flakes easily when tested with a fork, about 10 minutes.

SALMON MOUSSE

1 tbsp. unflavored gelatin
¼ c. cold water
1 tsp. salt
1 tsp. dried mustard
¼ to ½ c. vinegar
2 egg yolks, beaten
1 lb. salmon, flaked
2 tbsp. horseradish
¾ c. chopped celery
½ c. whipping cream
sliced olives or pimento
    or both if preferred

Dissolve gelatin in cold water. Mix salt and mustard thoroughly. Add to vinegar and egg yolks in double boiler. Stir constantly and cook until thick. Remove from heat and add gelatin. Stir until dissolved. Add horseradish. Chill mixture. Whip cream. Mix salmon and celery, add to gelatin mixture and fold in cream. Place olive pieces in bottom of oiled loaf pan or fish mold. Arrange mixture on top, pack lightly. Chill until firm. Unmold onto tray and garnish.

Garnishes: Hard cooked eggs - sliced
Sliced cucumber - with peel
Tomato wedges
Watercress, etc.

CRISPY BATTER
(for fish)

1 c. all purpose flour	2 tsp. sugar
2 tsp. baking powder	1 tbsp. salad oil
1¼ tsp. salt	1 c. water

Mix and sift dry ingredients. Add oil to water. Make a well in the dry ingredients and slowly pour in liquid, stirring until well blended. Makes enough for 2 lbs. of fish.

JAPANESE FISH BALLS

1½ lb. fish fillets	1 tbsp. soya sauce
1 c. water chestnuts, bamboo shoots, or bean sprouts	1 tbsp. vegetable oil
	¼ lb. fat pork or bacon
	1 c. blanched almonds
1 tbsp. preserved ginger	2 tbsp. cornstarch

Sweet and Sour Sauce:

¾ c. canned pineapple juice	½ c. sugar
½ c. vinegar	⅓ c. chopped green onions
1 tbsp. soya sauce	⅓ c. strips of green pepper
½ c. water	⅓ c. canned pineapple chunks, well drained
3 tbsp. cornstarch	

Grind fish in food grinder or blender or "double chop" it with 2 knives very fine. Grind pork and add to fish. Coarsely chop the chestnuts. Finely chop the ginger and almonds. Add to fish. Blend in soya sauce, cornstarch, and oil. Shape into flat small cakes or 1 inch balls. Fry about 3 minutes in deep fat heated to 375 degrees F. or fry in a shallow amount of oil in fry pan until golden brown on all sides. Serve hot with Sweet and Sour Sauce.

To make Sauce: In a saucepan combine juice, vinegar soya sauce and half the water. Heat to boiling point. Blend cornstarch and sugar with remaining water. Stir into sauce and cook, stir till sauce is clear and thickened. Just before serving, add vegetables and pineapple. Keep sauce warm on low heat so vegetables don't cook.

FISH CANAPE SUGGESTIONS

Salt cod fish in strips.

Slices of smoked salmon or halibut (flitch) on toast.

Square of marinated herring on small slices of raw onion set on a cracker or toast, garnished with a tiny pickled red pepper.

Hot Tuna Canape: Mix flaked tuna with mayonnaise or salad dressing, add chopped stuffed olives. Season with Worcestershire sauce. Spread on toast strips, sprinkle with grated American cheese. Place under broiler unit or burner until cheese is melted. Serve hot.

Salmon and Egg Canape: Blend hard-cooked egg yolks, flaked salmon and mayonnaise or salad dressing to smooth paste. Toast sliced bread squares on one side. Spread salmon mixture on untoasted side. Garnish with chopped parsley and hard-cooked egg white.

Anchovy curls or filets on toast fingers, edges dipped in mayonnaise and then sieved egg yolks, garnished with strips of pimento.

Tiny baking powder biscuits and tiny cream puff shells filled with lobster or any chopped fish mixture and serve hot.

Whole shrimp set on a small cracker which has been spread with tartar sauce colored green.

Potato chips topped with chopped lobster moistened with Russian dressing.

SALMON BRAISED IN BEER

2 lbs. salmon
1 tbsp. butter
1 c. beer
1 bay leaf
1 tsp. peppercorns

1 carrot, thinly sliced
1 onion, thinly sliced

Place fish in a buttered baking dish. Add remaining ingredients. Cover dish with buttered aluminum foil. Bake 20 min. until fish flakes easily. Transfer salmon to a serving dish. Serve hot or cold. (Preheat oven to 300 degrees F.) Serves 4.

SHRIMP CREOLE

2 green peppers, chopped
Salt and pepper to taste
1 bay leaf

2 lbs. boiled shrimp
1½ c. tomatoes
1 lge. white onion, chopped

Place in buttered casserole with tomatoes, chopped onion and green peppers. Bake about ½ to 1 hr. in moderate oven, about 300 degrees F.

Canning & Miscellaneous

CANNING & MISCELLANEOUS

CANNED FISH LIKE YOU BUY

You can use almost any kind of fish for this. Perch is excellent. Wash and clean thoroughly. Cut in thick slices and pack into clean sterile sealers. Large bones may be removed. For each qt. sealer prepare the following:

    1 tsp. salt   1 tsp. dry mustard
    Pinch of pepper   2 tbsp. vinegar
    6 tbsp. vegetable oil

Mix salt, pepper and mustard and sprinkle over fish. Add vinegar and salad oil. Adjust the rubbers and caps on the jars. Seal tightly, then unscrew a quarter turn. Set the sealers on a rack in a wash boiler or canner and cover with hot water. Bring to the boiling point and boil steadily for 6 hours, replacing the water as it boils away. Remove the sealers one a time and tighten the caps. Cool slowly. Store in a cool dry place.

Note: Do not pack fish in the sealers too tightly or fill too full. Set sealers upright when removing from canner.

CANNED TROUT

Clean and cut fish into pieces. Soak fish for 1 hr. in brine made of 1 c. salt dissolved in 1 gal. cold water. Place clean plate on fish to keep fish under brine. (use brine only once). Drain fish for several min., then pack fish into clean jars, place skin side next to jar and leave 1 inch of head space. Add ½ tsp. salt and ½ tbsp. vinegar to each pint, 1 tsp. salt and 1 tbsp. vinegar to each quart. The vinegar softens the bones so they can be eaten along with the flesh of the fish. Put on tin lids that have been in boiling water, then screw band down tight. PRESSURE COOKER METHOD - process pints and quarts at 10 lbs. pressure for 100 min. BOILING WATER BATH - process pints and quarts 240 min. Keep jars covered with boiling water and count time from the time the water started to boil. Heat for 10 min. at boiling temperature in stew pot before eating. Fish is just as good precooked before canning. I fry the pieces in bacon grease and this gives a nice flavor.

CANNED FISH

Fill quart sealer ⅔ full of freshly washed cut up fish. Add 1½ tsp. salt, 3 tbsp. pure vinegar and ¼ c. tomato ketchup to each jar. Fill to top with fish and seal

* EXTRA RECIPES *

tight. Process 3 hrs. after water has started to boil. Keep jars under water. Take canner off stove, but leave jars in water until it has cooled. Remove jars and wipe dry.

VENISON MINCE MEAT

5 pts. ground meat
   (boil until tender)
1 pint suet
2 c. currants or raisins
2 or 3 pints white sugar
2 tbsp. nutmeg
2 tsp. salt

10 pt. chopped apples
1 pt. vinegar
2 pts. raisins
1 lb. (2 c.) brown sugar
2 tbsp. cinnamon
2 tbsp. cloves

Citron or mace if desired. Use fruit juice for moisture, cook slowly for 1 hr. or so. Can while hot. Yields - about 7 qts.

HOW TO CAN OR PRESERVE WILD GAME WHILE OUT IN THE WOODS

Fry steak from any wild game and put in jars, or crock then boil up fat or lard and pour over meat until meat is covered. You can also roast meat and put in jars or crock and do the same. Meat will keep for months this way as long as you keep it covered with fat.

TO CAN MEATS

Canned meat is best if cooked before putting into jars. Leg bones, ribs and meat scraps should be boiled until it can easily be taken from the bones. Cook roasts as you would any roast. Season to salt and pepper whether boiled or roasted. Cut all meat into small pieces. Put into jars leaving 1 inch of head space. Pour the water from the meat that was boiled over the meat in the jars leaving 1 inch head space. Done this way all your jars will jell. The more bones used the firmer the jelly. Be sure to use tin lids and bands and screw them tight before processing. PRESSURE COOKER METHOD - process pints 1 hr. and 15 min. at 10 lbs. pressure. Process quarts 1 hr. and 15 min. at 10 lb. pressure. BOILING WATER METHOD - process all jars of meat 210 min. counting time from when water boils around the jars. The water should cover the jars while processing by adding boiling water. Never add cold or warm water as this will stop the boiling. All meats and fish can be canned raw but is much better if precooked before being put into jars. I often put 1 tbsp. vinegar in each quarts of meat if there are any tough pieces.

MEAT STEW OR GOULASH CANNED

Beef, pork, chicken, rabbit or turkey can be used. Precook to remove bones.

4 to 5 lbs. meat
3 c. chopped celery
3 qts. cubed, pared potatoes
   (about 12 med.)
1½ tbsp. salt
½ tsp. pepper

2 qts. diced carrots
   (about 16)
3 c. chopped onions
1 tsp. thyme

Cut meat into 1 to 1½" cubes. Brown in skillet in a small amount of bacon fat. Combine meat, vegetables and seasonings. Cover with boiling water. Pack hot into hot, well sterilized jars leaving 1 inch head space. Put on sterilized tin lids and band. Screw tight. Yields - about 7 quarts. Vegetables do not need to be precooked. Pressure cooked process pints 1 hr. Pressure cooker process quarts 1 hr. 15 min. at 10 lbs. Boiling Water Bath method process pints or quarts 210 min. Keep jars covered and count from the time the water starts to boil.

VENISON MINCE MEAT

3 c. chopped, cooked
   venison or moose
2 c. currants
1 c. chopped suet
2 c. sugar
1 tsp. nutmeg
½ tsp. cloves
2 c. diced apples
2 c. chopped seeded raisins

1 c. finely chopped citron
2 tsp. salt
2 c. cider or fruit juice
1 tsp. cinnamon
1 c. meat stock

Cook venison and cool in stock. Put venison through a coarse food chopper. Mix ingredients in order given. Simmer 1 hr. Seal in hot, sterilized jars. This makes 5 pints.

BROWN SUGAR SALT CURE

Stir until dissolved -
   ⅓ c. brown sugar
   ⅔ c. pickling salt

1½ qts. water

Layer meat or fish in solution. Let stand 4 hrs. for fish, small chunks or moose 2½ to 3 hrs. Remove from solution. Place on rack and let drain. Smoke.

TO CORN BEEF

Cheaper cuts of meat can be used. Brisket, chuck plate or rump.

    25 lbs. beef   2 lbs. pickling, dairy or
    1 lb. sugar   kocher salt
    1 oz. saltpetre   1½ tsp. baking soda
       (sodium nitrate)

Cut meat into pieces 3 to 6" thick. Put thin layer of salt in bottom of stone crock or tight keg, add layer of meat, sprinkle with salt and add another layer of meat and sprinkle salt over it ending with a layer of salt. Let stand 12 to 18 hrs. in a cool place. Dissolve sugar, soda and saltpetre in a quart of lukewarm water, mix with 3 qts. cool water, pour over meat. Cover with dinner plate or glass pie plate. Place clean rock gently onto plate to hold plate below the top of the brine. Meat must be kept under the brine at all times. Scum should be removed each day. The meat is ready to use in 3 or 4 weeks. It will be a bright red colour. (If brine ferments, drain and wash meat. Wash container and scald, prepare new brine and return meat to crock and pour new brine over it). Corned beef can be kept for several weeks if checked every day or can be canned.

MEAT BRINE FOR DEER OR MOOSE

    2 c. coarse pickling salt   1 c. brown sugar
    2 tsp. black pepper   2 tsp. baking soda
    ½ tsp. saltpetre

Cut meat and sprinkle each piece lightly on all sides, with mixture. Pack lightly in crock and weigh done the lid. Store in cool place, watching to see that the meat is always covered with brine. In 5 to 7 days meat is ready for cooking or whatever.

HOW TO CURE WILD MEAT

    7 lbs. elk shoulder   1 c. brown sugar
    2 gallons water   2 tbsp. saltpetre
    6 c. salt

Trim off all fat, bone and roll meat. Wash in cold water. Boil the 2 gallons of water, add salt, sugar and saltpetre. Cool. Place meat in earthen ware crock. Pour over brine. Top with a plate that will hold the meat down in the brine. Cover with waxed paper and then a clean tea towel. Leave meat in cold place, for 10 days to 2 weeks, depending on size of the piece of meat. Turn the meat often. If brine becomes spoiled, drain off liquid, wash meat carefully and cover with a new brine. Rinse in cold water, then soak in cold water overnight. Simmer in water or barbeque sauce and for using the canned elk in a chilled loaf.

CANNED CO-HO SALMON

fresh salmon
salt water
1 tsp. salt
2 tbsp. Ketchup

2 drops tabasco sauce
1/8 tsp. garlic salt
1 tsp. butter or cooking oil

Clean and skin fresh salmon and cut into chunks. Soak in salt water for 24 hours. Drain, wipe dry and pack into quart jars, 1 inch from the top. Add salt, ketchup, tabasco sauce, garlic salt and butter. Seal and process in pressure canner at 10 lbs. pressure for 1 hour, 40 minutes or 4 hours in water bath.

PRESERVING MUSHROOMS
(ESPECIALLY MORELS)

To preserve wild mushrooms, especially morels, slice them in half lengthwise; rinse them off; lay them on a cookie sheet while still wet and then place them in the freezer for 1 hr. or longer. Fill plastic freezer bags with these little morsels, each frozen in its own individual ice jacket and replace in the freezer until needed. Thaw and drain on absorbent paper towels before frying. They taste like they were just picked. Can be kept up to 9 months.

BLOOD SAUSAGE

Use pork-half lean and half fat. I use meat from the head, also pork heart and tongue can be used. Boil meat so it's not too well done so when it's ground, it stays in chunks. Grind with a coarse grinder. Add salt and ground allspice to taste or flavor. I use less allspice and add a little black pepper; use flour depending on amount you are making, to thicken or set sausage. After it's put in casings, boil sausage to thicken in casing. Prick casing while cooking to let out air. Do not let water come to boiling as sausage could burst. Just keep near boiling.

PICKLED FISH

Takes 2 weeks.
    5/8 c. salt
    White cider vinegar
    Fillet fish into bite-size pieces

After the 5 days:
    Onions (how ever many you like)

Cover fish with following cold pickle solution:
    1 qt. distilled white vinegar
    2 c. sugar
    5/8 oz. pickling spice

Skin and fillet and cut fish into bite-size pieces. Place in large earthen crock or a 2 gal. wide mouth glass jar. Add 5/8 c. salt for each qt. of cut up fish. Cover fish with white cider vinegar and let stand for 5 days in the fridge. After 5 days, rinse fish; cover with cold water and let stand ½ hr. Drain and pack pieces loosely into pint jars, alternating with layers of sliced onions. Cover fish with the following cold pickle solution: 1 qt. distilled white vinegar. 2 c. sugar and 5/8 oz. pickling spice.
Covers jars; let stand for 1 week. Keep refrigerated. After 1 week, it may be eaten from the jars.

PICKLED FISH

    1 qt. white vinegar   1 tbsp. pickling spices
    Salt and pepper to taste

Place fish in liquid. Bring to boil. Boil for 5 mins; remove from burner. Put fish, sliced onions and lemon (sliced), in container in layers. Put liquid back on stove and bring to boil. Pour over fish and let set for 2-3 days.

SMOKED FISH

Wash fish in salt water and dry. Brush with melted butter. Sprinkle with celery salt inside and out. Put in very warm smoker until you can pull the dorsel fin out. Cover the coals with hardwood sawdust. Smoke for 1-1½ hrs. Eat while still warm.

PASTIES

Filling:

1½ lb. steak, cubed (round or sirloin)	½ tsp. salt
3 c. potatoes, sliced thin	¼ tsp. pepper
½ c. finely grated carrot or rutabaga	1 tbsp. butter
½ c. chopped onion	¼ tsp. Accent, if on hand

Crust:

3 c. flour	pinch of salt
⅓ c. vegetable shortening	⅓ c. water

Mix cubes of steak, potatoes, carrot (or rutabaga) and onion together in a large bowl. Add salt and pepper. Don't allow to stand too long, otherwise potatoes will turn dark. Set aside.

Make crust, using flour, shortening and salt. Mix well. Gradually mix in water using a fork. Pat together into one ball. Divide into smaller balls and roll the dough out to the size of an 8 inch pie tin.

Baking: Place 1 c. mixed filling on half of a rolled crust; fold over and seal edges. Brush with milk and bake at 475 degrees for 20 minutes. Reduce heat to 375 degrees and heat 30 additional minutes.
GOOD EATING!!!!!!

BANNOCK

2¾ c. flour	2 tsp. baking powder
½ tsp. salt	4 tbsp. lard
⅔ c. water	

Sift, then measure flour; resift with baking powder and salt. Cut in lard to form fine crumbs. Gradually add water. Turn out on lightly floured board, knead 10 seconds. Grease heavy cast iron pan. Flatten dough to fit pan. Place on grill over hot coals. Cook 8 minutes or until bottom is lightly browned. Turn and brown other side. Cut in wedges and serve hot with butter. Yield: 6 to 8 servings.

BANNOCK CAMPFIRE BREAD

4 c. flour
8 tsp. baking powder
About 3 c. cold water
1 tsp. salt
1 tbsp. sugar

Mix the ingredients thoroughly and stir in enough water to make a thick batter that will pour out level. Mix rapidly with spoon until smooth. Pour out into large greased fry pan, set on hot coals. Turn when bottom part is brown. Or put greased Dutch oven on coals and rake the coals up around the sides. Pour batter into this and put on the lid. Cook till no dough sticks to a sliver of wood stuck into it. This can also be cooked in a greased pan in the oven. Bake 45 min. at 400 degrees.

HOMEMADE GRANOLA

2½ c. old fashioned rolled oats
1 c. shredded coconut
½ c. coarsely chopped almonds
½ c. sesame seeds
½ c. shelled sunflower seeds
½ c. unsweetened wheat germ
½ c. honey
¼ c. cooking oil   1 c. raisins

Roast rolled oats for 15 mins. in baking pan. In large bowl combine oats, shredded coconut, almonds, sesame seeds, sunflower seeds and wheat germ. Bring honey and oil to a boil. Stir into oat mixture. Spread out in 13x9x2 baking pan.

Bake in 300 degree oven until light golden brown, 30 to 40 min. stirring every 15 min. Remove from oven, stir in raisins (a mixture of dried apricots, chopped dates and raisins may be used). Stir occasionally during cooling to prevent lumping. Store in jars or plastic bags. To store granola more than 2 weeks, seal bags and freeze. Makes 6½ c.

TOFFEE PULL

January is a great month for getting together for a toffee pull. Here is a basic recipe that should provide indoor fun for those cold wintery days.

Part I:
Mix together and cook until it forms a hard ball in cold water (250 degrees F. or 122 degress C.).

    2 c. white sugar   ¼ c. vinegar
    1 c. corn syrup   ½ tsp. salt
    ¾ c. cold water   ¾ tsp. cream of tartar
    Add 1 tbsp. butter   1 tsp. vanilla

Part II:
Cool saucepan in cold water until candy is firm enough to handle. Take about ½ c. of candy and pull between well-buttered fingers. Bring back together and pull until toffee starts to clear. Pull into a rope or desired thickness. Twist and allow to set. Break into pieces when hard. Have fun!

Sourdough

SOURDOUGH

STARTER

      2 c. warm water into container - add 1 pkg. active dried yeast OR
      1 yeast cake OR
      1 level tbsp. dried yeast
ADD - 2 c. of white flour

Mix these ingredients to form smooth paste, leave lid loose fitting, then place the container in warm place overnight or longer if a more tangy flavour is desired, twenty-four hours at least is recommended. By this time the SOURDOUGH MIXTURE will be made up of small bubbles and should give off a pleasant alcoholic aroma.

This SOURDOUGH STARTER can be kept in the refrigerator as long as you replenish what is taken out for baking. (If the STARTER is not to be used for several weeks it can be frozen or dried to keep it from spoiling. In the dried form, the yeast goes into a spore stage, which is like dried yeast will keep for a long time. Water and warmth bring the yeast back to an active stage.) While in the refrigerator the low temperature will cause the bubbles to disappear and a clear liquid will rise to the surface - this is normal. Just stir before using. (Alaskan prospectors and Indians would skim this liquid from the top, ferment it and use it as alcoholic liquor).

Each time you wish to use your STARTER you must first pour out 1 c. of STARTER and set it aside as a STARTER for the next baking effort. This cup of STARTER is then returned to the container and the amount taken out is replenished by adding flour and warm water - NOTHING ELSE. The mixture will improve with time and once the fermentation is under way this cup of STARTER will be sufficient to sour the flour overnight. Let it work in the pot for at least a day before storing in refrigerator.

WHITE SOURDOUGH BREAD - OVERNIGHT SPONGE METHOD

With this method one is able to obtain the amount of sour taste preferred. In this recipe set the SPONGE going the night before bread is to be made. Put 1 c. of the SOURDOUGH STARTER into the mixing bowl. Add 2½ c. of flour - stir in lightly. Add 2 c. of WARM WATER 95 degrees F.

Mix this thoroughly. Dough might be lumpy, but this will break down. Cover with cloth, or piece of plastic (as a bread bag) would do the job better. Place in a WARM spot overnight (at least for 12 hrs.) It is important dough is kept warm at all times.

When you are ready to begin to make bread remember to replenish (in the pot) the STARTER you removed for the baking purpose. THIS IS IMPORTANT, THIS IS YOUR STARTER FOR THE NEXT TIME YOU WANT TO MAKE YOUR SOURDOUGH BREAD.

Now to commence making your bread:

IMPORTANT POINTS:

Warm kitchen, warm flour, froth up yeast separately. Suggested size bread tin for 1 lb. of dough 8x4x3" deep.

Ingredients required:

1 c. of water - 100°F.	Add the yeast and sugar to
1 packet of active dried yeast	the warm water (in a larger container than the 1 c. size
or	to allow for expansion)
1 yeast cake	Stir until broken down,
or	this will start your yeast
1 tbsp. active dried yeast	working almost immediately
½ tbsp. sugar	

2 tbsp. of butter or shortening
1½ tbsp. of sugar
2 level tsp. salt
4 c. of white flour
¼ tsp. baking soda

Add this to your SPONGE in your mixing bowl. Just stir in, then add yeast and continue mixing, adding flour if necessary until too stiff to continue mixing with spoon. Turn out on the floured board. Knead with hands, again adding more flour if needed to make a light smooth dough. Have the finished dough softer rather than stiff.

Lightly grease your mixing bowl. Place in dough, cover with cloth (plastic is better) and let rise in warm place until double in bulk. Knead briefly. Divide dough into pieces (to half fill your baking tins) fold into the shape of a loaf, using very little flour on your dough when folding. Place in warm greased tins, OR shape round and place on greased cooking sheet. brush over with melted butter or salad oil, put in a warm place. (example - warm place - put the oven on to WARM for a few., turn the oven off) then place bread on rack cover with cloth, and leave until dough reaches about the top of the tin or doubled in size if rounded up on cookie sheet. Now remove from warm oven. Turn the oven up to 425 degrees F. then when the oven reaches this temperature return loaves and bake for about 5 min. at this temperature, reduce temperature to

350 degrees F. and bake for about 20 to 25 min or until bread is loose from the sides of the pan. When baked, turn out the loaves to cook on wire grid or towel. For a soft crust brush tops of bread with butter.

IMPORTANT POINTS:
If bread is not allowed to rise (proof) sufficiently before baking it will be heavy or very close texture.

If allowed to rise (proof) too high, loaf will be spongy and will dry out quickly. The correct proofing will come with experience.

SOURDOUGH ROLLS

(KEEP THE DOUGH WARM AT ALL STAGES)

Prepare the dough the same as for your SOURDOUGH BREAD but add - 1 tbsp. shortening AND 1 tbsp. of sugar. Shape into rolls OR roll out dough to ¾" thickness, cut to the desired shapes, place a little apart on a lightly greased baking pan. Put in a warm place to rise (proof) to about double in size. Bake for about 20 min. at 400 degrees F.

SOURDOUGH TINNED BREAD

1 c. SOURDOUGH STARTER
2½ c. warm water
5 c. unsifted flour

Mix together thoroughly in large bowl. Cover with cloth or plastic and leave overnight or at least 12 hrs. in warm place, before proceeding with next step.

2 tbsp. cooking oil OR melted shortening
1 tbsp. salt
2 tbsp. sugar
2 tbsp. baking soda

Mix these ingredients together and stir until well mixed.

2½ c. unsifted flour

Add to above mix by hand to bring together then turn on to bread board or counter top and knead until the dough is smooth. Add more flour if needed but do not have dough stiff. Divide and shape into loaves. Place in warm greased bread tins. (suggested size bread tins for 1 lb. dough 8x4x3" deep). Let rise (proof) in warm place until nearly double in size, 2 to 4 hrs. Brush with melted butter. Bake in preheated oven 5 min. at 425 degrees F. then reduce the heat to 350 degrees F. and bake for another 25 to 30 min.

SOURDOUGH BREAD STICKS

Make up dough as for SOURDOUGH BREAD, divide into 4 pieces. Roll each ball out between the hands, outwards, on floured board. As you roll dough out it will tend to spring back, so roll out until dough toughens. Let rest for a few min., then dough should be relazed. Continue rolling to make them cylindrical and about ½" thick, cut to the length required, brush with water and place about 1" apart on lightly greased cookie sheet. Set in a warm place to rise, bake in hot oven 400 degrees F. for about 15 min. or until brown and crispy.

VARIETIES: After washing bread sticks with water, press sticks on coarse salt, poppy seeds, garlic salt, sesame seeds, caraway seeds, onion salt.

OLDE COUNTRY RYE BREAD - WITH SOURDOUGH

SOURDOUGH SPONGE:
    2 c. rye flour
    ½ tsp. honey or brown sugar
    1 c. warm water

Before using the making bread, keep in a glass container at room temperature for about 1 week.

BREAD:
    12 c. rye flour
    2 tsp. honey or granulated sugar
    3 pkg. of dried yeast
    About 5 c. warm water
    2 c. SOURDOUGH SPONGE

Mix the yeast, honey, or granulated sugar with 1 c. of water at 95 degrees F. to commence fermentation.

Put the 12 c. of rye flour along with the 2 c. of sour dough in mixing bowl. Add about 5 c. of the warm water. Add the yeast. Knead for about 5 min. (Experience will tell you if the dough is too wet or too dry). Let the dough rise in the bowl, in a warm place, for about 2 hrs. Now knead again thoroughly. This dough will handle differently to white bread dough. It will be softer and stickier. Ladle the dough into bread pans ¾ full. Smooth the top of the dough with wet hands. Let rise for about ¾ hr. Have the oven at 400 degrees F. Bake for about 40 min. This bread will be quite solid but this is characteristic of Olde Country type Rye bread. The addition of caraway seed imparts a delightful flavor to this bread.

WANT SOMETHING MORE INTERESTING THAN BACON AND EGGS FOR BREAKFAST.

SOURDOUGH HOTCAKES — PANCAKES

THE TRADITIONAL YUKON BREAKFAST IS SOURDOUGH HOTCAKES IS FAMOUS FOR ITS DELIGHTFUL FLAVOUR AND GOOD NOURISHMENT.

BATTER:

Take 1 c. of your SOURDOUGH STARTER, place in your mixing bowl (pottery or glass or stainless steel). Add 2 c. of warm water and 2½ c. of flour. Mix thoroughly cover with wax paper or plastic. Set in warm place overnight (about 12 hrs.). Take out 1 c. of the batter, put into container as your starter for the next baking, before taking the next step. When ready to commence making hotcakes add to your batter:

¼ c. of warm milk
1 tsp. salt
½ tsp. baking soda

2 tbsp. melted shortening or cooking oil

Mix together, then add 1 egg. Do not beat, but, mix well. Let stand about 10 min., then fry in a LIGHTLY greased HOT frying pan. Use 1 tbsp. of batter for each pancake.

MORE DELICIOUS VARIETIES OF PANCAKES CAN BE MADE BY EXPERIMENTING. HERE ARE A FEW VARIATIONS TO HELP YOU -ALL FROM BASIC BATTER.

BACON - sprinkle diced bacon over the batter after it has been spooned into the pan, on to the uncooked side before turning.

HAM - add ½ c. chopped ham over batter after being spooned into pan.

CHEESE - add grated cheese over top.

APPLE - add chopped or grated apples and sprinkle a little cinnamon or nutmeg over batter after it has been spooned into pan before turning.

BANANA - slice thinly - place on top of batter after it has been spooned into the pan.

BLUEBERRY - drop on top of batter after it has been spooned into the pan.

SOURDOUGH - WHOLE WHEAT - HOTCAKES, PANCAKES
THESE ARE DELICIOUS

MAKE A SEPARATE STARTER FOR THE FOLLOWING AS YOU CANNOT TAKE OFF THE ONE CUP TO ADD TO YOUR BASIC STARTER, AS THIS WOULD SPOIL IT.

STARTER:

Mix together - 1 c. whole wheat flour
      1 c. warm water
      1 pkg. yeast

Let stand for about 12 hrs. in a warm room covered with wax paper or plastic. Then carry on as for white flour pancakes. Your batter for whole wheat pancakes may be on the thick side, if so, it can be thinned with extra warm milk. Batter for pancakes should then be thin.

WHEAT GERM: Substitute 1 c. of wheat germ for 1 c. of flour in the basic recipe.

OATMEAL: Substitute 1 c. of oatmeal for 1 c. of flour in basic recipe.

CORNMEAL: Substitute ½ c. yellow cornmeal for ½ c. flour in the basic recipe. These will be crispy and crunchy.

SOURDOUGH MUFFINS #1

Set your sponge as for hotcakes in mixing bowl the night before you want to use it. When ready for baking take out your one cup for next STARTER.

Mix together and stir into your overnight sponge:

   2 eggs
   ½ c. cooking oil or soft shortening

Then sift into the above mixture:

1½ c. whole wheat flour
½ c. of non-fat dried milk
½ c. sugar
½ tsp. salt   1 c. raisins or chopped dates
1 tsp. baking soda

and stir just enough to moisten the flour. Fill greased muffin tins about ¾ full and bake at 375 degrees F. for about 35 min. or until baked. Yields - about 1 doz.

SOURDOUGH MUFFINS #2

2 c. whole wheat flour
½ c. soft butter or shortening
½ c. sugar

Mix the following ingredients together for better distribution through the mix.

2 tbsp. molassses   ¾ tsp. baking soda
½ c. milk

1 c. raisins or chopped dates

Mix together the above ingredients, then add enough STARTER to hold the mix together (start with about ¾ c.) mix lightly. Fill greased muffin tins ¾ full, and bake at 375 degrees F. in pre-heated oven, for about 35 min. Yields about 1 dozen muffins.

SOURDOUGH DEVILS FOOD CAKE

(CHOCOLATE CAKE)

1½ c. sugar ⅔ c. shortening	Cream together in large bowl or electric mixer
3 eggs	Add one at a time, beating thoroughly between each addition
1 c. Starter	Add to the above and blend in.
1¾ c. flour	Sift

½ c. cocoa   Add to above alternately with

½ tsp. baking powder

1 tsp. salt

1 tsp. cinnamon

¾ c. water
1½ tsp. soda   mixed together
1 tsp. vanilla

FROSTING FOR CHOCOLATE CAKE:

½ c. butter or margarine   Cream well

3½ c. of icing sugar   Sift together - add gradually
2 tbsp. cocoa   while creaming

Add enough milk (evaporated milk for preference) to make mixture right consistency for spreading.

SOURDOUGH DATE LOAF

½ c. of starter   2 tbsp. sugar
1 c. of evaporated milk   1½ c. flour

Combine these ingredients and leave at room temperature overnight.

½ c. quick cooking   ½ tsp. salt
   rolled oats   ½ tsp. cinnamon or allspice
1 tsp. baking powder   2 eggs, beaten
½ tsp. baking soda

Mix together and then add to the overnight sourdough mixture.

Finally add -
   1 c. chopped dates   ½ c. walnut pieces

Stir well, spoon into well greased loaf cake pan about 5x9x2½" deep; place walnuts on top and let stand for 1 hr. Bake in preheated oven at 375 degrees for about 1 hr. Let cool in pan for few min. before placing on cooling rack.

SOURDOUGH BANANA CAKE

½ c. shortening	Cream together
1 c. brown sugar	then add
1 egg	continue creaming for a few min.
1 c. mashed banana and 1 c. sourdough starter	Stir into the above mixture
2 c. all purpose flour 1 tsp. baking powder 1 tsp. salt ½ tsp. soda	Sift these ingredients add to the above mixture then add

½ c. of chopped walnuts and mix until just blended

Spoon into well greased and floured loaf cake pan, 5x9x2½" and bake in preheated oven 350 degrees for about 1 hr.

SOURDOUGH SPICE CAKE

½ c. sugar 1¼ c. shortening	Cream together
2 eggs	add one at a time beating well between each addition
1 c. of sourdough starter	blend in
1½ c. all purpose flour	
½ tsp. salt	Sift together
½ tsp. cinnamon or allspice	Add to the above
¼ tsp. nutmeg	ALTERNATELY WITH
1/8 tsp. cloves	
½ c. milk	mixed together
1 tsp. baking soda	

then add

½ c. raisins or walnut pieces

Mix well. Spoon into loaf cake pan 9x5x2½'' or a 9'' square pan.

Looking for a different dessert - taste the distinctive tang of:

SOURDOUGH WAFFLES

Batter:
>   1 c. sourdough starter   Beat well - let stand overnight
>   2 c. warm water
>   2 c. flour

Take our 1 c. of this mixture for the next batch, before proceeding to the next stage.

>   1 egg   Blend together
>   1 tsp. baking soda
>   1 tsp. salt   **THEN ADD**
>   2 tsp. sugar

>   5 tbsp. melted shortening or cooking oil - mix well until smooth

Pour a spoonful of batter into each section of a HOT waffle iron - bake until brown.

Tea Refreshments for 300 people:

12 large sandwich loaves, sliced lengthwise (6 white & 6 brown).

Fillings For Fancy Sandwiches

Ribbon & Rolled:

4 dozen eggs — hard boil, make filling with salad dressing and seasoning.

4 tins Klik or 1 lb. of ham or bologna — Mix with salad dressing and dills, chopped or sweet relish. This can be use for rolled sandwiches or ribbon type with egg using alternate layers of white and brown bread.

1½ lbs. white cream cheese — Mix with salad dressing. Spread on bread. Sprinkle with chopped maraschino cherries. Make in rolls. Takes 1 - 12 oz. jar red cherries and 1 - 6 oz. green.

1½ lbs. Velveeta — Mix with salad dressing. Make in rolls with olive (takes about 4 per slice) or dill slices.

3 tins shrimp — Mix with salad dressing. Roll.

2 large tins salmon — Mix with chopped celery, salad dressing and seasoning. Roll centred with dill.

These should be tightly rolled in wax paper and refrigerated till cut. These amounts will make 800 sandwiches allowing 2-3 per person.

Dainties for 300 people:

3 per person usually allowed. 25 persons supplying 3 dozen each should be sufficient if a group project.

Also required: 2 lbs. tea
3 lbs. sugar cubes
3 qts. creamilk
½ gallon sweet pickles
½ gallon dills

SUPPER QUANTITY COOKING

BAKED BEANS FOR 100:

8 qts. dry beans
20 qts. salad
4 lbs. butter
4 qts. cream

4 lbs. salt pork
20 doz. rolls
20 pies
2 lbs. coffee

HASH SUPPER FOR 100:

40 lbs. corned beef
32 qts. potatoes
20 doz. rolls
20 qts. chopped cabbage

5 qts. salad dressing
4 lbs. butter
2 lbs. coffee
4 qts. cream

CABBAGE SALAD FOR 175:

20 lbs. cabbage
1½ qts. salad dressing

4 large cans crushed pineapple
2 bunches carrots

HAM SUPPER FOR 225:

48 lbs. canned ham
24 potato salads (solicited)
48 pkgs. peas (1 lb.)
5 lbs. coffee
9 qts. cream

45 qts. strawberries
6 pkgs. Bisquick (mixed re directions for shortcake)
6 qts. heavy cream

BRAISED BEEF FOR 200:

65 lbs. stew beef
60 lbs. potatoes
36 pies

Harvard beets
40 lbs. turnips
2 lbs. cheese

TURKEY DINNER FOR 250:

7 turkeys
75 lbs. butternut squash
20 large cranberry rings

75 lbs. potatoes
10 bunches celery
44 pies

CHICKEN SHORTCAKE FOR 135:

60 lbs. chicken
30 pkgs. frozen peas
12 cans cranberry sauce

3 large pkg. Bisquick
17 pkgs. Flakon corn mix
2 bunches celery

POISON ANTIDOTES AND FIRST AID

KEEP CALM – DO NOT PANIC – CALL HELP

EMERGENCY PHONE NUMBERS

Doctor's Office _____ Home _____

Rescue Squad _____ Police _____

Pharmacy _____ Hospital _____

Emergency Poison Control Center _____

See other side of this page for substances most frequently ingested by Children . . . .

* An emergency always exists if someone swallows poison. Do not delay contacting hospital or physician to obtain advice concerning first aid materials that are not readily available. If necessary, summon police or rescue squad for assistance. Keep telephone numbers immediately available. Even after emergency measures have been taken, always consult physician. A delayed reaction could be fatal.

* It is important to dilute or remove poisons as soon as possible. Sometimes Syrup of Ipecac (available from some Pharmacies or poison centers) is kept in the home to induce vomiting IF RECOMMENDED by physician, or indicated on product label. If Syrup of Ipecac is not available, try to make patient vomit by tickling back of throat with finger, spoon, or similar blunt object after giving water.

HOWEVER . . .
* Vomiting is NOT recommended in all cases. Never induce vomiting in a patient who is unconscious or convulsing. Do not induce vomiting if swallowed substance is acidic or corrosive or petroleum distillate products.

* If poison is from a container, take container with intact label to medical facility treating patient. If poisonous substance is a plant or other unlabeled substance, be prepared to identify suspected substance. Save evidence such as portions of ingested materials from vomitus which may help identify plant or object involved.

The following represent substances most frequently ingested by children, and first aid measures that may be employed until medical aid can be summoned.

Substance	Emergency treatment
MEDICINE (OVERDOSAGE)	
Aspirin and aspirin-containing medications	Give 2-3 glasses of water or milk, then induce vomiting UNLESS patient is unconscious or convulsing.
Cough medicine	Induce vomiting. Then give glass of milk.
Hormones (including thyroid preparations)	Induce vomiting. Do not induce vomiting or force fluids if patient is unconscious.
Vitamins and iron tablets	
Sleeping pills	
Tranquilizers	Induce vomiting unless patient is unconscious. Give 2 tablespoons epsom salts in 2 glasses of water.
HOUSEHOLD CLEANING AND POLISHING AGENTS	
Laundry bleach	
Automatic dishwasher detergents	Give 2-3 glasses of milk or water immediately. **Do not induce vomiting.**
Household cleaners	
Furniture polish	
Cleaning fluid (gasoline, kerosene)	
Charcoal fire starter	
Toilet bowl and drain cleaners	**Do not induce vomiting.** Give 2-3 glasses of milk or water at once. **Avoid** gas-forming carbonates and bicarbonates.
Wax remover	Give milk or water. **Do not induce vomiting.**
Fabric softeners	Give milk. Neutralize with **weak** soap (not detergent) solution. Induce vomiting.
Household ammonia	Give citrus juice or diluted (1 tablespoon per glassful) vinegar. Then give 2 raw egg whites or 2 oz. olive oil. **Do not induce vomiting.**

INSECTICIDES, POISON SUBSTANCES, PAINTS (Read labels for content)	
Arsenic	Give glass of milk immediately and induce vomiting. Then give activated charcoal (available from pharmacist).
DDT	Induce vomiting. Give 2 tablespoons epsom salts in 2 glasses water. **Do not induce vomiting.**
Lye	Give solution of vinegar (2 tablespoons vinegar in 2 glasses water). Next give 2 raw egg whites or 2 oz. olive oil.
Paint (dry)	Give milk or water. Induce vomiting.
Paint (liquid)	Give 2-3 glasses of milk or water. **Do not induce vomiting.**
COSMETICS	
Cologne or perfume	Give milk. Induce vomiting if large amounts ingested.
Hand lotion	
Liquid makeup	
Skin lotion	
After-shave lotion	
Deodorant	Give milk of magnesia. Induce vomiting.
Bubble bath liquid	Give milk or water at once. Induce vomiting.
Hair rinse (conditioners)	
Shampoo	
Nail polish and removers	Give milk. Induce vomiting.
Lacquers	
Bath oil	
Home permanent neutralizer	Give milk or water. Induce vomiting. Then give weak acid such as lemonade, citrus juice, diluted vinegar.
Permanent wave solution	
PLANTS	
Any plant is a potential poison.	Induce vomiting if convulsions not imminent. Give artificial respiration if nec-

THE ST. JOHN AMBULANCE
FIRST AID CHART

1. Don't panic — reassure casualty — have him lie down if possible.
2. If patient is not breathing, apply artificial respiration at once.
3. Stop severe bleeding at once.
4. Call or send for Doctor immediately.
5. Immobilize all fractures.
6. If patient unconscious, watch closely — give nothing by mouth.
7. Protect from harm, keep reasonably warm.
8. Examine for further injuries.

	HOW TO RECOGNIZE	DO THIS FIRST	FOLLOW WITH THIS FIRST AID TREATMENT	DON'T DO THIS
ASPHYXIA (no breathing)	Cause: electric shock, suffocation, drowning, strangulation. Patient's lips, nose, ears, fingernails, toes may be bluish-grey. Breathing may be difficult or may have stopped.	Remove cause from patient or patient from cause. Provide fresh air. For electric shock, turn off power, use protective measures to break contact. Open air passages. Remove any obstruction (dentures, gum, food).	Apply artificial respiration at once. (See below). Call a Doctor immediately. Have bystanders help with wet clothing, cover patient with blankets, call police, and fire rescue team if available.	DON'T touch anyone in contact with a live wire. DON'T enter a gas or smoke-filled room until protection or ventilation is assured. Never assume patient is dead. DON'T allow revived patient to drive or remain alone until checked by Doctor.
SEVERE BLEEDING	External: blood may spurt or flow steadily from wound. Internal: Indicated by bleeding from mouth, blood in urine, stool, swelling at site of fracture, internal pain, pallor, fast/weak pulse, restlessness, air hunger, thirst, clammy skin.	External: apply pressure directly on wound with thumb or fingers over a clean pad or dressing. Have patient sit or lie down, elevate injured part. Internal: have patient lie with feet raised 8", cover with blanket.	External: apply additional dressings, bandage firmly. If bleeding continues apply tighter bandage on top. Call Doctor. Internal: advise doctor and remove patient to hospital soonest. Give nothing by mouth.	DON'T waste time looking for special dressing, etc. STOP bleeding first. DON'T give stimulants until bleeding controlled. DON'T give alcohol. DON'T disturb blood clotting over a wound.
BROKEN BONES INJURIES TO JOINTS	Generally pain, deformity, loss of use, difficult breathing (ribs). Bone end may protrude through skin. Bleeding from ear indicates possible skull fracture. Numbness or paralysis of lower extremities indicates injury to spine.	Stop any bleeding. If possible do not move patient. Splint fracture carefully. If a joint is dislocated apply most comfortable position. For sprains apply cold water compresses. Place chest injury in best position for breathing.	Secure dislocations and splinted fractures in a sling or to chest or other leg. Bandage cold compress firmly to sprains. Notify doctor. If back injury suspected, get help, lift patient without bending neck or spine onto firm flat surfaces, pad body hollows.	DON'T move until necessary, particularly cases of head, spine and hip injury; and then move with adequate support and in most comfortable position. Never jackknife. DON'T remove clothing unless bleeding is present.
BURNS, SCALDS AND FROSTBITE	Cause: flame, hot metal, hot liquid, acid, sun, electricity, skin may be reddened, blistered, hard and yellowish or black with bleeding. Frostbite appears as waxy whitish area with loss of sensation — often unnoticed by victim.	Immerse superficial burns in cold water or apply frequent changes of cold wet towels. Guard against infection. Cover serious burns quickly with dry sterile dressing, sheeting, etc. Do not break blisters. Only First Aid treatment for frostbite: warm with body heat.	Maintain cold water treatment until patient relieved of pain. Keep otherwise comfortable. Give sips of warm drinks. Bandage serious burns to prevent infection and remove to medical care, and give nothing to drink: For acid or alkali burns; flood with water.	DON'T break blisters, or breathe on burns. DON'T put anything on serious burns, e.g., ointment, creams, etc. DON'T give anything by mouth in serious cases. DON'T hesitate to call Doctor re burns to children or elderly persons.
POISONING	Identify poison as soon as possible, notify Doctor or if not available, Poison Control Centre, immediately. Be able to inform doctor or hospital if possible, what poison was taken, quantity swallowed, how long previously, present condition of victim, location of victim and your phone number.	If victim has taken lye, drain cleaner, gasoline, kerosene, strong acids — DO NOT MAKE HIM VOMIT. Take the victim and a sample of the poison swallowed to hospital immediately. In case of delay in treatment give water or milk to dilute poison.	If victim has taken other poison give milk or water and make vomit by pressure of finger or spoon handle on back of tongue. Place victim's face down with head lower than hips when vomiting. Be sure to clear airway. Don't waste time inducing vomiting — get victim to hospital.	DON'T spend more than five minutes trying to get patient to vomit — if not successful get him to hospital. DON'T store poisons, medications, aspirins, detergents, solvents, acids, etc., where children can reach. DON'T take any medicine without first reading the label.

MISCELLANEOUS INJURIES AND CONDITIONS

MINOR WOUNDS: (SCRATCHES, ABRASIONS) Wash with soap and water. Cover with sterile dressing and bandage firmly to stop bleeding. See doctor if further treatment necessary.

POISON IVY, OAK, AND SUMAC: Wash affected part thoroughly with soap and water, dry, and swab with alcohol. Apply calomine lotion.

FOREIGN BODIES IN EAR: Fill ear with mineral or olive oil or water containing baking soda. If insect does not float free, consult Doctor.

IN EYE: If it can be seen and does not appear to be imbedded, gently remove foreign body with corner of clean handkerchief or tissue moistened with water. If no avail, cover eye and as with imbedded objects, seek medical aid. DO NOT RUB. For chemicals in eye, wash eye carefully with copious amounts of water for at least 20 minutes. Consult Doctor at once.

ANIMAL BITES: All animal bites should be treated as serious and a Doctor consulted immediately. If an animal is suspected of being rabid, it should be destroyed but the head saved for analysis. If the bite is from an apparently healthy animal, the animal should be impounded for seven days to make sure it does not develop symptoms of rabies. Keep bitten part low. Bathe wound in a weak solution of potassium permanganate.

STINGS AND INSECT BITES: Bathe with moist bicarbonate of soda or weak ammonia. If a bee stinger remains, don't squeeze, but scrape out of skin. Best prevention for mosquito, blackfly bites: preparations containing Diethyltolyamide. Use and store commercial herbicides and pesticides with extreme care. They are also poisonous to birds, animals, and humans.

HEAT EXHAUSTION: Symptoms include headache, dizziness, nausea, vomiting, sometimes abdominal cramp, collapse, and unconsciousness. The face is pale with cold clammy sweat. Pulse is weak. Temperature may be normal or slightly raised. Place casualty in cool place. If conscious, give cool salted water to drink (¼ tsp. per glass). Keep comfortably warm. Watch for any change in condition. If temperature rises rapidly, face becomes flushed, skin hot and dry and pulse full and bounding, patient is suffering from Heat Stroke. Immediately wrap patient in cool wet sheet and fan him. Temperature must be brought down to 102 degrees as soon as possible. When this is done, wrap patient in damp sheet and call doctor.

ARTIFICIAL RESPIRATION

WHEN BREATHING STOPS — LOSE NO TIME — EVERY SECOND COUNTS

DELAY CAN BE FATAL

POSITION OF CASUALTY: When rescued, place casualty on his back and raise shoulders with available clothing, blankets, etc. Tilt head well back in order to raise tongue off back of throat and open airway. Remove obvious obstruction with fingers by tilting head to side.

ORAL METHOD:

With one hand lift neck; with other press forehead back and pinch off nose. Seal off casualty's mouth with yours and blow sufficiently to make his chest rise.

Remove your mouth allowing air to exhale. Repeat cycle every 3-5 seconds until recovery. For children use smaller puffs more frequently.

MAKE SURE THE HEAD IS KEPT TILTED WELL BACK.

When you can't effectively seal off mouth, close mouth with one hand against chin, tilt head well back and blow through casualty's nose. For infants, cover both nose and mouth with your mouth.

Where casualty has been submerged in water, powered by earthfall or avalanche—administer first breaths as soon as face is uncovered.

SYLVESTER METHOD:

Kneeling astride casualty's head, grasp his arms at wrists. Cross them over lower half of his sternum and rocking forward, press firmly downward only sufficient to force air out of the lungs. This phase should take 2 seconds. Count "one and two and . . ." Release downward pressure, pull arms upward, outward and backwards. This extends the chest walls drawing air into lungs—PROVIDED THE AIRWAY IS KEPT OPEN BY ADEQUATE HEAD TILT. This phase should take 3 seconds, counting "three and four and five . . ." Return the wrists to the sternum for a continuation of the rhythmic cycle each 5 seconds, somewhat faster for a child.

CAUTION: adjust chest pressure to correspond with age and build of casualty.

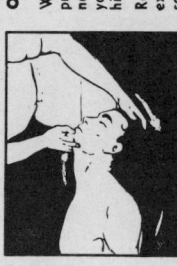

BE PREPARED

★

LEARN FIRST AID

★

KEEP YOUR FIRST-AID KIT UP TO DATE

LEASE CUT OUT AND MAIL CARD FOR INFORMATION

— — — — — — — **Canadian residents please use this one** — — — — — — —

Please send information on the *no risk, no investment* plan of publishing the project checked below.

Check one:
- ☐ PERSONALIZED COOK BOOK
- ☐ WILD GAME COOK BOOK
- ☐ COMMUNITY ACTIVITY CALENDAR
- ☐ PERSONAL HOCKEY MEMORIES
- ☐ PERSONAL BASEBALL MEMORIES
- ☐ FIGURE SKATING DIARY
- ☐ TOWN OR ACTIVITY BROCHURE

The information should go to: M _____

of _____
    Town   Province   Postal Code

Organization is _____

of _____
    Town   Province   Postal Code

My name is _____ of _____
                                                Town   Province

Phone _____ Date _____

CUT RIGHT ON LINES

— — — — — — — **U. S. residents please use this one** — — — — — — —

Please send information on the *no risk, no investment* plan of publishing the project checked below.

Check one:
- ☐ PERSONALIZED COOK BOOK
- ☐ WILD GAME COOK BOOK
- ☐ COMMUNITY ACTIVITY CALENDAR
- ☐ PERSONAL HOCKEY MEMORIES
- ☐ PERSONAL BASEBALL MEMORIES
- ☐ FIGURE SKATING DIARY
- ☐ TOWN OR ACTIVITY BROCHURE

The information should go to: M _____

of _____
    Town   State   Zip Code

Organization is _____

of _____
    Town   State   Zip Code

My name is _____ of _____
                                                Town   State

Phone _____ Date _____

Business Reply Mail

No Postage Stamp
Necessary if mailed
in Canada

Postage will be paid by

GATEWAY PUBLISHING CO. LTD.
811 Pandora Avenue West,
Box 220 Transcona P.O.
Winnipeg, Manitoba, Canada
R2C 2Z9

NO POSTAGE
NECESSARY
IF MAILED
IN THE
UNITED STATES

BUSINESS REPLY MAIL		
FIRST CLASS	PERMIT NO. 19046	MINNEAPOLIS, MINN.

POSTAGE WILL BE PAID BY ADDRESSEE:

GATEWAY FUND RAISING SYSTEMS INC.
117 North 2nd Street
Minneapolis, Minnesota 55401